Urban
Elements

By Bryan Wesley

POETRY........ Is emotion

intertwining with words & life experiences combined with the mind working together to craft an image or feeling that can be felt by millions upon millions of listeners & viewers? The creativity of poetry can be expressed in many ways & in many forms & has been around for many generations, it's a blessing to be blessed with such a gift to craft words with imagination it's about the art of poetry that matters most & it comes from your inner self so every time you write you write from the soul so whether you're on stage at the open mic or writing it on a sheet of paper give it your all.

Table of Contents

Chapter 1- Urban Community

Chapter 2- Essence of Love

Table of Contents

Chapter 3-Depression

Chapter 4-The Inspiration

Table of Contents

Chapter 5- Astrology

Chapter 6- Sex+ Intimacy + Passion

Table Of Contents

Chapter 7-Millennial Renaissance

Chapter 8- Classics Remastered

Table of Contents

Chapter 9- Success Ladder

Chapter 10- Expressions

Chapter 11- Journey of Life

Acknowledgments

A special Thank You to all the great poets who came before me

Maya Angelou

Gwendolyn Brooks

Countee Cullen

Nikki Giovanni

Langston Hughes

Robert Hayden

Forrest Hamer

Jupiter Hammon

Chapter One

Urban Community

~Homegrown~

You don't have to look far,
To find the next superstar,
One who rises & raises the bar,
Globally striving while others aren't on par,
Supreme demeanor,
Once a follower now a leader,
A visionary thinks beyond locally,
Worldwide takeover globally,
A dream & plan require action,
Fueled by passion,
Ignore hate & distraction,
You'll accomplish more than you can imagine,
Make it all happen,
There will be hate,
Some won't support or relate,
But don't let that stop you from being great,
Have faith,
Keep your eyes on the prize,
Remain positive & wise,
Climb the success ladder & rise,
Whether it's long nights or sweaty days,
Success can be attained in multiple ways,
They ignore you today, but tomorrow they praise,
Whether they ignore or throw shade,
Stay striving because you got it made,
Be rare & different from the rest,
So if you searching for the best,
Check your own backyard for talent & success.

~Empowerment~

Why kick you down when I can lend a helping hand,
Support you & help you establish a plan,
So you can,
Be a better woman & better man,
I don't understand,
Why be divided,
At war & misguided,
When we can be a powerful force,
On course,
To blissful peak,
Where we feel strong instead of weak,
Even at your lowest your still one of the elite,
Dear men feel my uplifting words,
Spread your wings & soar like birds,
Don't let one rejection,
Lead you to depression,
Cut from a different cloth you're the exception,
Set your goals high & reachable,
To those who doubt the unbelievable,
Man on a mission is truly unbeatable,
Dear ladies striving,
Never stop thriving,
Your star is rising,
As your blessings are arriving,
Keep your head up to the skies,
God needs to see your eyes,
Now focus on your prize,
Lift you up to the highest elevation,
Behold the next rising sensation,
Soaring past doubt & expectation,
Enjoy your success & celebration.

~ *All Lives Matter* ~

Below the surface,
Topics that make us uneasy or nervous,
No human race is worthless,
We all are born with a purpose,
No skin color is a disgrace,
There is no superior race,
We all strive to win,
We all sin,
But we should not be judged by our skin,
Let us stop the stereotype,
Never feed into the ignorant hype,
Let us think on our own,
Judging others is dead wrong,
No ignorance,
Stop the prejudiced violence,
Measure each human soul by substance,
Let's settle indifference,
 By using our intelligence,
Hate only fuels more hate,
Whether you're black or white we can all be great,
Speak only love & don't let ignorance spread,
Through the wars, disagreements & tears shed,
No matter the skin color we all bleed the color red.

~Lifestyle Change~

The life we live is a precious one,

Full of laughter, sadness & fun,

As we grow into our own,

We learn our surroundings & roam.

We learn just who we are,

Work ethic can take you from ordinary to superstar,

As kids we dream,

Day by day we are building our self-esteem.

Whether you're getting education or playing on a
Sports team,

Never lose sight,

The journey may take all day & night.

Eliminate negativity & stress,

Trust the process,

Be guided by prayer & progress,

Life is a gamble,

Full of internal battle,

As you travel,

Be sure to shake those crabs in a barrel.

Sometimes you got to just change your surroundings,

Change a few things,

You'll be surprised at what life brings.

All you got to do is believe,

Trust & knowledge you'll soon achieve,

Talk less & try to listen,

Make the best choice with ultimate precision,

It's your life so make the best decision.

~ *Self-Esteem Inefficiency* ~

The biggest qualities that are essential
that help us reach our full potential,
Start from the inside,
that very thing that shapes our dignity & pride,
that very thing that makes us feel alive,
it is our motivation & drive,
It is self-esteem,
it's what makes us a well-oiled machine,
for it is unseen,
but can have you feeling & reigning supreme,
But on the opposite end,
is an esteem that can't ascend,
feeling inferior like it can't contend,
can't evolve or transcend,
A lack of love for self,
isn't good for your health,
No need to feel low,
we are all destined to shine & glow,
it's our self we should get to know,
take our time & get our ducks in a row,

Stay in your lane,

play it smart & maintain,

campaign to get past the pain,

happiness is yours to gain,

blissful joy is easy to obtain,

let happiness reign,

Self-esteem is a reflection of you,

so always remain true,

nothing can measure up to your value.

~Code Red~

Where do we begin,

We have to look deeper than the skin,

Examine within,

We all make mistakes & sin,

We all love & hate,

We all living trying to get straight,

Love is a fundamental human trait,

Ignore the stereotypes allow each other to be great,

Don't box one another in,

Ignorance is the final nail in the coffin,

Use time to dedicate,

Learn & educate,

So we as people can relate,

So racial tension can deflate,

So we all can prosper & elevate,

We need more unity,

We need positive growth in the community,

Now is the perfect opportunity,

Instead of chaos & mutiny,

We can live together beautifully,

Life of extinguished quality,

United in harmony,

No false hope I speak prophecy,

No skin color is a disgrace,

Only race is the Human Race,

Let's embrace,

Blessings we'll soon receive,

We all trying to achieve,

We all cry, laugh & bleed,

We all struggle,

We all trying to survive & hustle,

Life can be a puzzle,

Allow love & peace to be widespread,

In the end we all bleed red.

~ It Takes A Village ~

Urban communities can be often wild,

Conditions often reckless nothing mild,

God Bless the child,

Parents establish the worth,

Knowledge stays with us till we buried under dirt,

Over the Years,

Kids spend more time with peers,

Community helping the youth conquer fears,

Even help establish careers,

Teachers are the guide,

Helping students in their educational stride,

Balanced with school pride,

with so much at stake,

it takes a village to mold someone great.

~ *Healthy Living* ~

Life is precious

we need to focus more on our wellness,

Balance our diet,

think more healthy minded,

We live in a fast food climate,

where "Have It Your Way" is provided,

Kids are getting bigger,

food got them looking thicker,

but who is to blame or where do we point the finger,

When ads are promoted by your latest Hip-hop

Singer,

When food is so convenient & cheap,

commercials poison minds like sheep,

Long term affects ain't nothing nice,

but healthy food is way over priced,

Jesus Christ,

But let's address the issue deeply,

we eat unhealthy not just daily,

But weekly, even against our own safety

sounds crazy,

but the food is unhealthy but tasty,

Instead of eating & drinking by the gallon,

let's take action,

Provide awareness & balance,

let's make something happen,

Instead of letting calories quadruple,

get active & become useful,

this healthy dose of knowledge is fruitful,

Can't argue the facts because it's truthful, so instead

of that burger with cheese,

understand the leading cause of death is Heart

Disease,

This isn't about making you skinny or dissing you if

you fat,

it's about getting your life back,

put down the snack,

hit the treadmill or run the track,

Start today because tomorrow isn't giving,

today start a healthy living.

~*Black Unicorn*~

Powerful beyond measure,
Calm & cool under pressure,
always striving for better,
It is fierce, original as a pioneer,
has no fear,
but let's make this clear,
It's not demanding,
it's crafting, building & establishing,
alluring & ravishing,
creating & branding,
not cocky but confident,
truly dominant,
creating a legacy lasting & prominent,
it's an annoyance,
to criticize the unicorn of flamboyance,
instead you should blessed by its appearance,
be captivated by its brilliance,
motivated by how it handles business,
be an eyewitness to how gifted & ambitious,
it finds the will to pursue its happiness,

Black isn't demeaning,
it isn't weird it's intriguing,
dreams are worth believing,
Black isn't toxic,
or demonic,
yes it's symbolic,
but varies in many meanings,
expressed in different feelings,
this is more than an overdue celebration,
due to rumors & speculation,
Black has a bad reputation,
Black is equal,
Black is powerful & peaceful,
the power lies in the people,
unity is truly masterful,
Black is truly powerful.

~ *Less Tea, More Milk* ~

Ratchets are always focused on the wrong,
in business they don't belong.
Ratchets have a bad attitude & short fuse,
Ratchets have ignorant views.
spreading false information live coverage & Breaking
News,
but when it comes to themselves they haven't got a
clue,
Always failing life lessons,
hating on others only block they blessings,
So much drama & mess they creating,
some people don't got time for hating,
Rather focus on checking & saving,
striving & maintaining,
Negative individuals are draining,
when it comes to negativity we need restraining.

This lifestyle is only for the hopeless,
a person handling they own business don't got time
to notice,
in your own lane is where you should focus,
Positive people aren't afraid,
to help people upgrade,
Milk isn't just good for your body & health,
it's replenishment of soul & wealth,
it's the nurturing refreshment,
life is about progress & advancement,
You can gossip & spill tea,
but being a quality individual is what you will never
be.

~Luxury & Privileges~

Time is never to be wasted,
your body is sacred,
he should feel blessed to see you naked,
for your love he should be dedicated,
you're a luxury that should be celebrated,
Worth more than gold,
a strong woman will never fold,
you get better with time & never get old,
The way you smile,
your ravishing style,
will have any lucky man running down the aisle,
any moment with you is worthwhile,
A luxury is a prized possession,
a man's weakness & obsession,
your worth more than a trophy in his collection,
your his one & only selection,
A valued prize,
in his eyes,
A treasure that steadily gets better,
powerful beyond measure,
worth all the passion & pleasure,
You are worth more than a fling,
you're a queen in need of a king,
Your standards never lower & you're very realistic,
never materialistic,
never any man's statistic,

sex is a privilege,
no woman wants century mileage,
no woman wants reputation damage,
so whether you speaking sexual language,
or carrying a large package,
a quality woman maintains her knowledge,
Valuing yourself is a curse & blessing,
but life is a lesson,
Cherish your health,
luxury is more than wealth,
it's value you place on yourself,
It's time to awaken,
a new dedication,
When it comes to sex you have no obligation,
ignore any complicated situation,
you're on the road to being a wise inspiration,
Your time is precious & your nobody property,
you're a privilege & a luxury.

~ *Community Uprising* ~

As a community we must think,

we are only as strong as our weakest link,

Tone down the gunfight,

bring positivity to the light,

this isn't about being black or white,

it's about remaining close & tight,

police our neighborhood by day & night,

let's do what's right,

Let's have a community conference,

to rid ourselves of the ignorance,

too much tolerance,

It's breaking us apart slowly,

pay attention closely,

we must stand united & boldly,

Be aware & be active,

love thy neighbor & forgive,

Why do we celebrate the wrong,

why can't we as a community be strong,

let's take our place where we rightfully belong,

The time is now,

here is how,

Let's uplift & feed our youth,

with nothing but knowledge & truth,

speak wisely never becoming mute,

ignorance isn't cute,

Put down the guns & uplift the test scores,

teach the youth that education opens up doors,

Be united as team,

teach the youth to dream,

to stay striving & never lose steam,

maintain high self-esteem,

Dear elegant ladies,

stay focused on raising those babies,

roof over the head,

clothes on the back & well fed,

Fellas provide protection & wisdom,

keep your kids out the system,

so your son or daughter will never be a victim,

Let's continue fighting,

educating & guiding,

community is now rising.

~The Gift~

Somethings go on & last forever,

knowledge is power & makes you better,

Words hold the ultimate ammunition,

that puts you in the perfect position,

Huddles will be overcame,

success you shall claim,

with the gift of knowledge you'll never be the same,

knowledge is game,

The gift spreads down through time like tradition,

conquering life toughest mission,

life can be stranger than fiction,

The gift should be shared with the youth,

wisdom & essentials of truth,

Knowledge passed down from generation to

generation,

the gift is a form of preservation,

life requires observation,

but the right decision need concentration,

but wrong choices teach us a wise lesson ,

Whether it's the future, past or present,

baby to teens & adolescent,

Knowledge is important to the body mind,

Faith & wisdom is your guideline,

the gift of knowledge will last a lifetime.

Chapter Two
Essence of Love

-

~ *Lovemaking Soundtrack* ~

Love is more than a feeling,

with multiple layers & meaning,

it can be sexual healing,

or you can be somebody sunshine,

maybe even be their boo or valentine,

Love only takes two,

Destiny Child says cater to you

sex doesn't have to be Fifty Shades of Grey,

you can get it on like Marvin Gaye,

or maybe you prefer R.Kelly 12 play,

sometimes words not need be said,

on any given holiday you can put your mate to bed,

it's no need to pretend,

but what if your just a friend

you thought there was a future & it would never end,

I wonder,

how can someone be a part time lover,

love can be a dilemma,

at odds & war how can she be your umbrella

one minute you addicted to her like a drug,

next minute you screaming I Need Love,

love can be a dead end or lead to a marriage
vow,

but the time is Here & Now,

whether they your bae or boo,

whether it's a crush on you,

doesn't matter if the feeling is big or small,

love is the greatest of all

relationships can be an emotional roller coaster

things can break you apart or pull you closer,

through any weather a couple must say

Let's Stay Together,

love is beautiful & that's a fact,

let life create your own beautiful lovemaking
soundtrack.

~ *Dynamic Relationships* ~

All relationships aren't created equal,

the world is filled with different kinds of people,

We all have a preference,

but we all separated by difference,

What we hold near & dear,

others may fear,

But the goal is to impress ourselves not our peers,

but some people question themselves for years,

Dynamic relationships is one we should cherish,

whether it's unforeseen or a fetish,

it's our life we have the right to embellish,

We have the right to create something special,

something remarkable on another level,

we need support & peers to be helpful,

Some people are closer than others,

true bonds overcome & conquers,

blood doesn't define you as partners,

Sometimes obstacles do,

sometimes an familiar mind gets you through,

Sometimes nobody understands,

the right person knows & the bond expands,

maybe this all apart of god's plans,
Something's are unexplainable,
but life is unpredictable,
but it all comes down to the principal,
being there for one another is pivotal,
some relationships aren't fixable,
while others haven't reached their pinnacle,
Relationships take a life of their own,
some are unknown,
one will never feel alone,
some people are your heart & backbone,
some relationships never reach a significant,
milestone,
These special types can't be categorized,
these relationships can't be jeopardized,
only recognized,
so to summarize,
A relationship this gigantic,
won't fall or sink like the titanic,
it will create magic,
forever will it be dynamic.

~ *Simple Things* ~

Everything doesn't revolve around money,
it's the time & effort that is most lovely,
Time is valuable,
it's about the times that are memorable,
funny & laughable,
it's a matter of simple tangibles,
Everything don't have to be mega,
something simple nothing extra,
There is nothing tragic, about something being basic,
nothing tops a classic,
We all have a variety of taste,
time is precious with no time to waste,
Comfortable is what people desire,
happiness is what we require
In life we search for things that are finer,
things that brighter & nicer,
whether it's major or minor,
With faith we strive much higher,
it's the simple things we acquire.

~ *Care Package* ~

This is no small token,
true words are more than spoken,
love is deeper than the ocean,
A care package is a deep devotion,
my passion is an explosion,
these words are more than a poem,
To explain our passions,
we must lead by our actions,
reward the person of our deepest attraction,
Pay attention & observe,
reward that person with a package they deserve,
Pay close attention
to the likes & dislikes plus the things they mention,
It's the effort that counts,
give your love in large amounts,
Gifts from shoes, clothes, & lingerie,
no matter the holiday,
every day will be your birthday,
Luxury satisfaction & five star meal,
to show how this love is real,
your special & get the package deal.

~ *Supreme Union* ~

It's sad when people to dictate,

your life your destiny & your fate,

when the ignorant question your faith,

instead of understanding they rather hate,

they pay close attention to your mate,

overanalyze if you gay or straight,

instead we should let each human be great,

Judging others when we need to sweep at our own
front door,

so many issues in America to address & restore,

so many issues & differences to explore,

seems like we a country at war,

but it's with thy neighbor,

America has always been about the paper,

we judge others preferences & failure,

but never should our rights be in danger,

love & equality should be in our nature,

we all should work to achieve greater,

the time is now not later,

Dispute the indifference,

nobody's happiness needs disturbance,

Promote love not ignorance,

provide a positive influence,

People have the right to love whomever,

never should love fold under pressure,

as a society & community let's get better,

No sin is greater than the next,

so as a community let's not hate or be perplexed,

Let's embrace,

love each other as a human race,

For months & years the oppressed prayed,

on June 26th history was made,

Some will comply & others will be overly holy,

live your life boldly,

Hold your loved ones closely,

preach equality & love only,

Love each other as human,

be your own supreme union.

~Infinity~

Nothing in life can compare or measure,

your my ultimate treasure,

give you affection & pleasure,

our relationship has grew even more better,

Words can't sum up my feelings,

my love has no ceilings,

We are inseparable,

your admirable,

if you stumble I'll never let you crumble,

together we remain unstoppable,

Whether it's hot sex,

or simply an I Love You Text,

Whether it's a look in your eye,

or my hand on your inner thigh,

I cannot lie,

I love you in more ways than words could explain,

from beginning to end my affection will remain,

the world might think I'm insane,

thru pleasure & pain,

I am not going nowhere,

a connection this strong is rare,

but I truly care,

In my eyes your incredible,

our shared experiences will never be regrettable,

your actions are respectable,

flawless your impeccable,

I love your eyes & how they glow,

make passionate sex to you like a pro,

lick you down from your head to toe,

Laugh together & cry together,

it's no pressure,

I love your soulful voice,

your top choice,

Your smile is blessed,

guide my hand down your breast,

then whisper in your ear that you the best,

Your laugh is cute & enchanting

this connection is everlasting,

Both our sports remain young

I love how you don't bite your tongue,

I love how you boldly speak,

I love you every day of the week,

one opportunity & I'll make you weak,

together we both will reach a new peak,
I love your independence,
I love being in your presence,
when you feeling down & want to cry,
I want to hold you & uplift you to the sky,
your spontaneous & always on the move,
every day you get better & improve,
not obsessed, just simply impressed,
true feelings should be expressed
you hurt I hurt,
you're the best thing on earth,
even if our dreams never come true,
I will forever love you, as a boo,
our strength is our unity,
truthfully I love you beautifully,
if our time come I'll never waste an opportunity,
love you to infinity.

~ *Romance Isn't Dead* ~

Romance is in critical condition,

what happened to the art of dating & tradition,

men & women aren't playing their position,

good men & women are getting props & recognition,

romance seems impacted by social media &

television,

Standards are at a record low,

relationships move fast no longer slow,

Some men don't know how to maintain a

conversation,

just straight sex & flirtation,

Dear god what's wrong with this generation,

people still in relationships way past their expiration,

Guys being lazy,

not knowing how to treat a lady,

calling every chick baby,

acting all kinds of shady,

What happened to candles lit & slow jams playing,

what happened to romantic experiences & love

making,

But fear not,

there are still people eloping & tying the knot,

There are people that take their time,

some men still wine & dine,

down to earth ladies are so divine,

There are still ladies with self-respect,

that will reject,

any man who comes at them incorrect,

there are ladies that are very direct,

Romance is alive & kicking,

romance is about vibe & building,

Giving an experience that will last an lifetime,

let romance set the pace & guideline,

Romance may not be what it used to be,

but it's still the key,

It will forever be optional love is possible,

romance is phenomenal.

~ *Emotional Breakdown* ~

Life can be crazy,

Downright scary,

Breakdowns happen,

Often caused by passion,

Built up pressure,

Causes ill-fated temper,

We all overreact,

In life we just trying to make an impact,

Odds stacked against your favor,

A blessing is a life saver,

In life we search for greater,

We just not trying to be a failure,

But the road gets tough,

But enough is enough,

Life is a game of chess,

There are tons of ways to beat the stress,

Success is yours to possess,

Don't over think,

Under pressure don't shrink,

Don't fold,

Be bold,

Bad times fade,

God & faith will be your aid,

Be self-made,

With God in your corner,

You'll forever be stronger,

Breakdowns you shall conquer,

Prepare for a new you,

It's time for your breakthrough.

~ *Husband Goals* ~

After the wild oats have been sown,
it's time to be grown,
It's time for the chickens to come home, to roost,
drama & games need to be reduced,
the grown man needs to be introduced,
saggy jeans replaced with suits,
a gentleman delivers truths,
a gentleman knows how to handle disputes,
It's all about progressing,
make sure love & knowledge is forever spreading
goals are required,
being a husband is the standard,
as a husband I will love & honor,
cherish my wife as my partner,
I will love & protect,
you're the Queen I respect,
Rub your feet,
never shall I cheat,
forever I'll remain romantic & sweet,
Make love endlessly,
marriage was our destiny,

I'll be proud to stand on one knee,

will you marry me,

Words I'll forever live by,

love is something you can't buy,

During your pregnancy,

I'll spoil you heavily,

being your husband is my specialty,

Rub your stomach & hear the baby kick,

nurture you when you sick,

as your water break,

I smile upon the journey that we getting ready to partake,

A bun in the oven,

is a blessing out of heaven,

But I'll be with you every step of the way,

as a husband I'll love you more each & every day,

Nurse you to recovery,

feed your favorites during your monthly,

Together we will raise supremacy,

together we'll build a legacy,

Be here forever through the highs & lows,

These are my husband goals.

~ *Love Triangle* ~

The heart doesn't lie,
but it's confused on two
one is beauty at its best,
the other personality out of this world.

I must confess,
they both deserve to know the truth,
God doesn't like ugly,
this situation is getting out of hand.

One calls & leaves a message,
the other texts & sends emojis
one is always on Facebook,
the other constantly on Twitter.

One is outgoing, the other laid back,
both bring out something different in me,
each possess different flaws,
both are quality ladies.

I got a big choice to make,
one is sweet, the other fun loving,
one has a bad attitude,
the other throws temper tantrums.

Love triangle are tough,
all parties involved should be careful,
no person is worth this amount of stress,
no man or woman deserves this.

I know what I must do,
the answer comes down to me,
go with what I know best,
I must choose myself.

By choosing me everyone wins,
the ladies hearts are spared,
my conscious is free,
in this triangle I choose me.

~ *Rhythm & Feeling* ~

What was it that attracted you to me,
just maybe,
it was my words that drove you crazy,

Could it be the way I lit up the stage,
became all the rage,
or you sensed I was wise for my age,

Is it because I aroused your mind,
stood out like one of a kind,
maybe you just respect my grind,

Relax & sit back,
I'm not spitting game to Mack,
just being myself cut me some slack,

I observe then read & react,
keep calm & remain tact,
I speak knowledge & fact,

Your beauty exceeds the scale,
grade A approved while others are stale,
I'm different from any other male.

Step into my poetry zone,
where I set the pace & tone,
I'm Larenze Tate & your my Nia long.

I'll act as your guide,
upon the monumental ride,
never will we lose stride.

You are not a victim,
you're a queen in my poetic kingdom
guided by my wisdom, follow my rhythm.

~Potential~

Beauty & outlook is skin deep,
it's what below the surface that counts,
Sometimes it's better to step back,
better then reviewing with an biased eye,
Potential comes down to opportunity,
but opportunity doesn't come easy,
At any rate,
we have the potential to fail or be great,
Opportunity for the taking why wait,
sometimes you just got to wait your turn,
sit back & learn,
Ignite that passion so it can burn,
to whom it may concern,
One thing overlooked with potential
everyone isn't successful,
Potential can be seen,
but hard to redeem,
potential merely remains a dream,
Potential sometimes can't be met,
opportunities given soon be decisions we regret,
Potential is often a prediction,
sometimes it's luck,
Sometimes it's the best choice,
sometimes it's your only option,
potential isn't in everybody.

~ **Enchanted Celibacy** ~

Your body is a temple,
it is sacred & to be respected,

To be loved & cherished beyond measure,
deeper then pleasure your body is ultimately special,

No man shall disrespect or dishonor,
instead he should feel blessed,

Your body equals your choice,
no man controls your temple,

You have the final word,
all he can do is respect your decision ,

No means no that's final,
a real woman knows her worth,

If he can't see past your body,
then he doesn't deserve you,

Celibacy is beautiful,
don't let anyone tell you different,

Nothing wrong with saving your body for your
husband,
it's nothing wrong with waiting for a ring,

Love for self-outweigh anything,
health & maturity is a must,

Forever remain enchanted,
as a woman your truly in a class by yourself.

~ *Green Light*~

Seduction begins with the slightest touch,

emotions overflow & butterflies swarm,

The slightest touch causes an eruption,

erogenous zones have no fences,

But the boundary line is respect,

attraction doesn't equal permission,

Seduction doesn't guarantee intercourse,

everything comes down to choice,

Consequences follow unwise decisions,

kissing on her neck doesn't give you the right,

forced entry isn't acceptable,

Red means stop,

no further can you go,

Boundaries come with penalties,

freedom isn't worth losing,

Respect is a must,

loose lips sink ships,

Gossip is spread among the ignorant,

overindulgence can backfire,

Kissing & touching causes things to escalate,

but sometimes things just aren't ready to happen,

The heat of the moment can flame out,

one moment can change a lifetime,

A whole night can be ruined,

disrespect is a turnoff of epic proportions,

We travel at the speed of life,

but we must know when to slow our pace,

Yellow means slow down,

you may be doing everything right & perfect,

But the mood isn't there,

being comfortable is relaxing,

A woman has the right to change her mind at any
given time,

let relaxation kick in before warming up,

Green means all systems go,

you earn a pass,

your access has been granted.

~A Great Friend~

Associates turn up, friends uplift,
great friends are the ultimate gift,

A great friend is there thru the wrong & right,
A great friend will pull up on site,

A great friend can be of the opposite gender,
A great friend makes you better,

A great friend doesn't hate,
They help each other be great,

A great friend is dependable,
A great bond is incredible,

A great friend comforts,
The only destination is upwards,

A great friend speaks on your mistakes,
A great friend does everything it takes,

A great friend has great intentions,
A bond between great friends always strengthens,

During a crisis a great friend never withdraws,
A great friend recognizes your flaws,

Two great friends may clash & fight,
But in the end they always make things right,

Friends help you keep your sanity,
Great friends turn into family,

A great friend isn't seasonal,
thru the struggle, a great friend won't let you
crumble,

A great friend shows great care,
A great friend is rare,

A great friend love will get you through thick & thin,
A great friend helps you win.

Chapter Three
Depression

~Cupids Resentment ~

Why do things go the way they go,
why is it so hard for the relationship to grow,
Why can't bae do right,
I wish it was history that we could rewrite ,
where is Cupids arrow,
or why not shoot me with love bullets that are hollow,
why does bae bring so much misery & sorrow,
like the great men & women before them why can't
they follow
why is pride so hard to swallow
maybe Cupid will have something better for us
tomorrow,
where is the love,
why is there more pushing & shoving & less kiss &
hug,
why do our expectations come up short,
where is Cupids support ,
when it comes to love why are we the last resort,
is Cupid angry,
why won't Cupid shoot me to make me happy,
where is the one I'm going marry

where is the love & excitement
instead it's only resentment,
maybe cupid doesn't see any hope,
love & lust has always been a slippery slope,
people can fake relationships like orgasms,
relationships have more chaos & tantrums,
seems like friends with benefits last longer,
relationships use to be treasure now it's torture,
as we look back upon reflection
maybe this is progression
maybe next time we'll make a better selection,
maybe it's not cupid we should trust,
the value is in us.

~ *Post Breakup Depression* ~

What on earth can describe this feeling,

feels like your heart has escaped your body,

Your soul is dying slowly but surely,

head & body ache,

Expectations & life outlook is completely shot,

sadness seems permanent on your face,

You hate the opposite gender,

now you never want to be in a relationship ever

again,

Now you're thinking about being bisexual,

anything to cleanse yourself of pain,

But time is key,

depression is only in your mind,

The pain of a breakup soon passes like the wind,

time heals our deepest wounds,

Your days today may feel like sorrow,

but soon your sun will rise,

Then happiness will stay on your face,

resist the urge to text,

resist the urge to call,

delete them from your social media,

After a breakup it's time to focus on yourself ,

no looking back or having regrets,

no bitterness no hate filled heart,

Only growth & possession,

relationships teach us what we don't want,

experience is life best teacher.

~ *Food Chain* ~

Whether your top shelf or upper echelon,

faster than a Cheetah running a marathon,

poisonous strike like a Python,

There must be order & establishment,

some things are simply brilliant,

Struggle to the top will have its fair share of

frustrations,

dispute life complications,

some will arise to the occasion,

In life you have people at the top,

you have a cream of the crop,

from a work ethic that's nonstop,

Happiness & hustle with both its no telling what

doors you unlock,

Once your number one,

the job isn't done,

Your now a target,

you must remain guarded,

your now the most wanted,

Everyone is coming for your position,

no matter your circumstances or condition,

You will forever be in competition,

on the food chain you have a pack in the middle,

One notch lower but still skillful,

the dreams & outlook is wishful,

but a reign at the top is blissful

The journey won't be perfect,

but the grind is something they will respect,

after success then it's time to reflect,

But let us not forget,

down below the food chain lies a bigger threat,

The rise to stardom,

often starts at the bottom,

like a flower that blossom

success is awesome,

When the going gets tough,

the only way to go is up,

This is god's work so this isn't luck,

deep within yourself you'll found inner trust,

Success is something we all aim to gain,

dispute the struggle & pain,

raise supremacy on the food chain.

~ *Slut Shaming* ~

We say we hate promiscuous ladies,
but we always say "Where The Hoes At"

We put these ladies down for being overly sexually
active,
but high five a guy for smashing multiple ladies,

We get mad when they make us wait,
then put them down to the lowest degree if we get
the sex too soon,

We refuse upgrade our queens,
but downgrade them with no regret,

Treat them like dirt,
but we expect our mothers & sisters to get treated
with nothing but love,

The madness must stop,
we must unite not be divided,

Women are not Thots or sluts,
but princesses & queens,

Why put you to shame,
when I can simply praise.

~Crawl~

We have to follow before we can lead,
achievement & success is a process,
Rome wasn't built in a day,
only place success comes before work is the
dictionary,

Improvements over time lead to substantial growth,
complacency leads to disappointments,
evolution is the next phase,
work ethic separates the mediocre from the great,

Before you reach the mountain top,
you must fight your way thru the valley,
success isn't easy,

The feeling of accomplishment is incredible,
standing on your own feet is remarkable,
beginning steps to milestones,

As the pressure mounts,
cheers get louder,
devil gets busy,
God works harder,
family prays,
friends support,
before we walk we must learn to crawl.

~*Character Assassination*~

Things are more than meets the eye,

we all can leave a lasting impact before we die,

it just takes effort to try,

Happiness comes from within,

no human is without sin,

but some characters love to pretend,

authentic is a word some can't comprehend,

some characters are based on the latest trend,

Those below you are always in search of opportunity,

to drag you thru the mud brutally,

it's no unity,

especially when your under criticism & scrutiny,

People will build you up just to tear you apart,

testing your heart,

so you always got to play smart,

Be humble thru every congratulation,

some are hoping & wishing for your assassination,

Character evolves as our destiny is fulfilled,

you can't destroy something you didn't help build.

~Friendship Among Chaos~

It's hard to pick sides,

when you close friends with both,

you love them both to death,

But there is a rotten apple amongst them,

that rotten apple is causing friction & turmoil never
seen before,

that rotten apple is trying to have its way & more,

cake & then some,

It's like tornado it doesn't care who it harms in its
way,

love is a two way street,

Love requires the effort of two,

but lies can destroy tons of built up trust,

Lies can destroy a relationship,

not playing your position can cause destruction,

What do you do if both your friends are at each other
necks,

fighting for something that isn't worth it,

fighting for a spot that isn't meaningful,

So much drama & mess,

all because of the rotten apple in the middle,

one friend is hurt ,

the other friend feels betrayed,

the rotten apple feels superior,

I feel at a loss for words,

situationships shouldn't equal hardships,

thru chaos someone must maintain reason,

Someone must speak the truth,

we all need a friend to the rescue,

Thru chaos the real separate themselves from the deceitful,

Friendship thru chaos can be maintained,

people just got to do right.

~Eye For an Eye~

Karma comes in many forms,
in life expect the unexpected,
Life throws us sunshine, rain & storms,
every human life should be respected,

There is no higher worth,
we all have destiny,
We are all special to someone since birth,
mastering life & trying to create a legacy,

Human life holds special value,
choices teach us much knowledge
Heaven is our final resting venue,
each day we given is a blessing & privilege,

Family going to always seek justice,
past is never at rest,
Marching & showing up in bunches
loved ones going to show up & protest,

You take a life of someone close,
that is someone child, son or even mother,
Life returns the karma in a double dose,
we as a people supposed to love one another,

We all have one life to live,
losing a loved one hurts at the inner core,
Hardest thing to do is forgive,
family & friends are going to always try to even the score,

Karma catches up sooner or later,
love & live life till the day you die,
Life always returns the favor,
we all get served eye for an eye.

~*Spoiled Rotten*~

Everything that glitters isn't gold,
don't believe everything your told,

The best people are often shy,
there is more to them than meets the eye,

No human is perfect,
we all got flaws to correct,

Even milk looks good based on sight,
but if it's past expiration it won't taste right,

First impressions are overrated,
getting to know someone is understated,

It's all about what's on the interior,
personality is way superior,

Ladies it's not about the biggest bag,
blessings skip over those that brag,

You can dress down fully with luxury & price,
but quality is measured by more than price,

It's not about your shoes or being materialistic,
it's about quality & being realistic,

Fellas it's not about the biggest rim or nicest car,
it's about knowing who you are,
striving & getting far,

With the success we have or the times we suffer,
when life is over we all end up 6 feet under,

Character matters,
it's one of the many key factors,
in life you will meet many pretenders & actors,

It's not what's on the outside,
it's not about swag or pride,
it's not about the insecurities we hide,

Purity of the soul is what we should explore,
personality we shouldn't ignore,
what's pleasing to the eye is often rotten to the core.

~Sea of Mediocrity~

We have our moments life where we get down,
we crumble to our knees,
Depression rips us to shreds & makes us lose hope,
no matter what we do nothing seems to go right,
We seek help but nobody comes,
struggles pile on top on one another,
We try to wash our sins away,
thru it all we seem stuck in a sea of mediocrity,
it's hard to dream when you only see nightmare,
it's hard to see victory when you know is losing,
it's hard to gain momentum when it seems like you stuck,
it's hard to think positive when your surrounded by negativity,
Often times we are a byproduct of what we see,
experience is life cruelest teacher,
we start off at the bottom first,
then gradually move in a positive direction,
The only path is up,
when you use to failure you rarely know what success taste like,
We must cleanse ourselves of negativity,
change our mindset to focus on positive,
Destiny awaits us,
let's get out of the sea of mediocrity,
then submerge ourselves in positivity.

~Dead End Relationships~

The saddest sight to watch,
is a relationship on its last legs,
past its prime,
Struggling to make it last,
as you can grow together you can also grow apart,
Some people try hard while others not at all,
relationships require 100% effort from both parties,
How can you fight if the other refuses to get in the ring,
Trust is gone,
love is no longer existent,
sex no longer meaningful,
you can be in a relationship & still feel alone,
Some people use relationships for benefits only,
it's sad when the good days are far behind you,
it's hard to ride it out to the end when the tires are flat,
it's always best for both parties to go for their own happiness,
The relationship has ran its course
in the end maybe a breakup is for the best.

~After Effects~

After any situation,
some of us go thru liberation,
gain knowledge & information,
during the process of transformation,
we reevaluate ourselves thru exploration,
even go thru acts of desperation,

Life is a process,
with issues to address,

It's all about your reaction,
aftermath you got to gain traction,
tread carefully thru any distraction,

Aftermath can decide your fate,
but it can't keep you from being great,
you can progress at your own rate,

Others aren't as fortunate,
their motivation plummet,
a comeback isn't always definite,

Some never get back on their feet,

some can't handle the pressure or heat,

after effects leave them like road kill on the street,

What was lost can be found,

what knocks you to the ground,

can't keep you down, you can rebound,

Rise to the top can be something worth celebrating

coming up short can be devastating.

~Just Ride~

When trouble seems to double,
before you stumble & things crumble
remain humble,

Under so much stress,
caught up in drama or mess,
got feelings you can't express,

You don't want to be at home,
you don't want to speak on the phone,
you surely don't want to be alone,

You want someone that's going be here,
to cheer, better yet to get you thru fear,
shoulder to cry on & listening ear,

It's better to just ride,
maintain your pride, let your intuition be your guide,
travel thru neighborhoods or be city wide

Better to get in the car,
travel destinations that comfortable & far,
cruise & sit back looking at a star,

With a true companion you can't lose,
just ride & check out the views
night life exploring so just cruise,

Just ride it's a journey between you & the road,
just ride & let the stress unload,
relax & get in chilling mode,
moving to the beat of your own drum,
just ride & travel to see where you came from,
see where you came so you know what you could
possibly become,

Just ride for any amount of time,
ride till the sun set or the moon shine,

Stressed out to the max,
park & relax,

Some people go for a walk,
some even talk,

Life is a battle that we all fight to survive,
thru it all we can thrive,
if you need space just ride.

~*Buyer Remorse*~

Life comes with many regrets,

but rarely do we get a redo,

Rarely do we get second chance,

we can't time travel back to the past,

We get caught up in the moment,

see what we want & require,

Only to regret later down the line,

so caught up in the now,

The future of tomorrow gets ignored,

people only sell you dreams,

Quality & character sold separately,

we buy what we want,

Forget what we actually need,

relationships are the same way,

In the beginning you get your pennies worth,

towards the end it's never lived up to the hype,

Now you have remorse,

people selling dreams we buying them,

The only thing we get is regrets,

life is like a coin,

you only get to spent it once ,

even holy people have an asking price,

love don't cost a thing,

But it's hard to have romance without finance,

it's often quality vs quantity,

merchandise doesn't always age gracefully,

Maybe it's our expectations,

maybe we penny pinching,

something's in life you can't refund,

We got to make the best of what we have,

enjoy the gift of the present.

~Black Sheep~

The one people doubt,

in a bunch there is that odd one that stands out,

Often the one that is forgotten,

surely not spoiled rotten,

but definitely the last option,

Thru history black sheep carry negative implications,

dispute their negative reputation,

but black sheep are the ones that rise to the

occasion,

They go unnoticed,

moves & actions are the boldest,

black sheep go hardest,

even if their the oddest,

humble confidence keeps them modest,

Stereotyped as deviant,

black sheep always try to make a statement,

never caring about their placement,

black sheep don't care about your judgement ,

They too busy in their own zone,

making their presence known,

They don't care if their stigmatized,

talked about & criticized

having their every move analyzed,

their confidence can't be demoralized,

They know their great in every way,

they strive & work hard every day,

dispute what everyone say,

Their unique,

truly have a magical mystique,

don't sleep on the black sheep,

the one that transcends & takes momentous leap,

Black sheep you're not ordinary,

you stand above all as extraordinary.

Chapter Four

The Inspiration

~Still Standing~

Knocked down but still breathing,
beaten but the heart still ticking,
Overlooked but still working hard,
strength isn't about size,
The measure of a man is how he handle adversity,
will you stand down or stand up,
will you run or will you fight for what you deserve,
Defeat is your motivation to get better,
develop an appetite for success,
Come up short or stand tall,
downgrade or strive to move up,
Confidence is key,
perseverance is a must,
in yourself you must believe,
Never doubt the heart of a champion,
you got to shift into that extra gear to evolve,
Life isn't always easy,
hard times will happen,
overcoming obstacles is critical,
Victory begins with you,
losing is not an option,
The only option is to work harder,
stare fear in the eye & never back down,
If you fall next step is to rise,
stumble but maintain balance,
thru it all be the one still standing.

~Insecurity Adjustment~

Every person on earth has an insecurity,
this is a flaw we must correct quickly,
We either get better or worst day by day,
it's got to be a better way,
no matter the role we try to portray,
our insecurities will find a way to display,
that's not okay,
In ourselves we got to reexamine,
take action,
make the best of anything happen,
May take weeks, months or years,
get support from your peers,
till a new you appears,
Insecurities effect life in many areas,
Rarely are these events hilarious,
insecurities can cause us to be envious,
can make us feel alone & emptiness,
Can also affect our relationships,
ruin partnerships,
Can be a nuisance,
but hey we only human,
Cause devastation in our lives,
cause us to harm our wives,
Cause us to be tense & extra,
insecurities affect both genders vice versa,
Girlfriends with trust issues,
more insecurities then virtues,

dispute it being a new day the argument continues,
Time together not trusting the interactions,
it's only so much you can take with a person
imperfections,
Not trusting friends or family,
in an insecure mind your always guilty,
You suffer from the consequences of others,
an insecure mind always wonders,
Boyfriends being overly protective,
often with an insecure motive,
cause arguments that are explosive,
subject matter in nature is sensitive,
Judging you based on their past,
insecurities cause relationships not to last,
with an insecure person the attraction fades fast,
Insecurities can be bad for your health,
saying mean & cruel things that feel heart felt,
improvements are good for health,
With time your insecurities will be adjusted,
a new & improved you will be constructed.

~The More, The Merrier~

Thru the cycle of life,

you meet many people,

Some alike & some different,

but it will be that one soul,

that separates themselves from the pack,

that's an inspiration to everyone they surround,

This person has heart,

displays patience & leadership,

dignity & self-respect,

Independent & working towards a blessed lifestyle,

with God as guide,

This person is fun to be around,

live & full of creative spirit,

you maintain your faith & courage,

Cool & relaxed thru difficult moments,

you fight your way thru adversity,

Made the impossible logical,

weathered the mightiest storm,

Thru out your bouts you had God in your corner,

you're a blessing to every one you touch in life,

you're a friend that is truly remarkable,

Your pure in heart & pure in soul,

your smiles lights up the darkest room,

wish there was more like you on this planet,

The world would be much better,

these individuals are god's gift to earth,

This person deserves to be acknowledged for their
effort,

you're an inspiration & truly one of a kind,

the more of you the merrier.

~When Hell Freezes Over~

Being overlooked gets old,

no longer will you fold,

you will take action & be bold,

you have a reputation to uphold,

you don't rebuild you reload,

even if you have to travel alone down the road,

As we get older we get wiser,

obstacles go from hard to lighter,

difficulties become minor,

our rank goes much more higher,

Will you give in,

less talking & more walking,

you won't stop till the casket close on your coffin

Success can be an obsession,

we won't stop till it's in our possession,

Nothing comes to those who are lazy,

with persistence isn't no such thing as maybe,

you got a choice to grind daily,

or sit back & be scary,

Will you be afraid,

hesitate to upgrade,

Maybe when pigs fly,

maybe when Orange is the color of the sky,

be successful or die,

confidence is a must no time to be timid or shy,

Even when you down on your luck,

will you give up,

Destination is getting closer,

you truly are a fighting soldier,

you won't stop till you dead or hell freezes over.

~Legacy Continues~

Take some time to rejuvenate,
rest up to grind harder,

Dreams soon become reality,
every day is an opportunity to get a step closer to
your dreams,

Don't waste precious time,
after greatness comes relaxation,

But before greatest can exist,
struggle & triumph must happen,

Your drive defines your legacy,
you can choose to stop or continue,

No need to whine or complain,
get back to business & takeover,

No what ifs or would of, could of, should of,
only seek destroy & conquer,

Work hard to create a name for yourself,
a legacy is a forever lasting imprint,

Consistency will build the ultimate foundation,
the only place success comes before work is the
dictionary,

Be a visionary with a purpose,
not watching sitting back full of criticism & self-hate,

Your legacy your choice,
you define yourself.

~Equal Duty~

Ugliest thing on earth is discrimination,

nothing comes between a woman & her

determination,

Nothing is more admirable then a lady fighting for

her nation,

dispute the any males flirtation,

the many offers & temptation,

A lady's motivation,

is her ultimate foundation,

Sometimes is love from family or a friend,

the ones who care till the very end,

Anything a man can do,

women can too,

Strength is in both sexes,

there is no measure to what a woman possesses,

The issue has been ignored long enough time to

spread awareness,

time to promote fairness,

to those who are careless,

Promote ignorance,

a woman in duty is precious,

She isn't a sex toy,

she isn't a piece of meat just for you to enjoy,

She isn't your hoe or freak,

she is a woman who is unique,

can compete with any man any day of the week,

Equality is a fair compromise,

women can shoot, fight & exercise,

Women are often the smartest in the group,

work the hardest in group,

There is no doubt,

you ladies make us proud,

Every woman has a mission & goal,

getting mistreated gets old,

nobody can measure the strength in a woman's soul,

Ladies want unity & things to be peaceful,

ladies are useful,

brutal but truthful,

Fights for people,

women should be equal,

Ladies it's no need to overlooked or humiliated,

thru it all ladies you are appreciated.

~Caterpillar To Butterflies~

There comes a time,
where we must evolve to new heights,

We must crawl before we walk,
follow before we can lead,

Learn before we can apply,
master before we can achieve,

We must recognize our own capabilities,
analyze our strength & weakness,

We must undergo a process,
evolution of self,

Our thoughts shape our life,
our actions set the pace,

Time waits for nobody,
precious moments we must seize today,

Maturity is the next step in life,
wisdom is gained thru learning & experience,

Never should we fear transformation,
change is a great thing,

We all develop at our own pace,
some never mature at all,

Today you walk,
tomorrow you soar to a new beginning.

~Pure Excellence ~

Born a cancer in July,
first born to symbolize the leader you are,

Growing up wise & smart,
gentle with a loving heart,

Your truly special,
caring & gentle,
highly imaginative,
actions aggressive & conservative,

2008 was the year,
my life shifted into a new gear,
I met a friend who was near,
very kind & sincere,
from the beginning,
something great was building,
you keep on progressing,
you're a blessing,
thick & thin thru any solution,
in my life you're an excellent contribution,
I witnessed your evolution,
your precious as your favorite pearl,
I wouldn't trade you for anything in the world,

You're an individual who is loyal,
deeply devoted & emotional,

Tenacious with your goals,
multitasking great individual with a great head above
on your shoulders

you have matured into an pure hearted person

You are Determined
You are Incredible
You are Optimistic
You are Noble
You are Dedicated
You are Rare,
You are Amazing

~*Poetic Princess*~

Let's start this relationship from scratch,
I've finally met my match
our poetic hearts attach,
you're the perfect catch,

Our words intertwine,
there is great compatibility among our sign,
flow & rhythm like a perfect rhyme,
for your love I will wine & dine,

We connect emotionally,
express our views openly,
match made so heavenly,
we both have a love of poetry,

Many may compare,
but this is a love that we only share,
I truly love & I truly care,
this is a love that is rare,

A poetic love we both comprehend,
I can't lie or pretend,
love the time we spend,
let our love ascend,
connected by the love of the pen,
love you to the very end.

~*Blessing in Disguise*~

Situations take on a life of their very own,
situations won't always go according to plan,

Life has many questions,
God has many answers,

Remain positive both in mind & spirit,
God works in mysterious ways,

Our purpose isn't always clear & precise,
God has a bigger plan for us,

God doesn't make mistakes,
he simply makes adjustments & corrections,

When life seems stormy today,
a blessing in disguise awaits.

~Less Tears, More Smiles~

Dispute your biggest disappointment,

it's time to make a big adjustment,

time for better judgement ,

with God almighty as your consultant,

less tears is the goal,

happiness is something you control,

happiness you should never relinquish,

your self-esteem should never diminish,

emotional scars are only a small blemish,

with love of self you got to be selfish

no matter what goes horribly

your happiness is a top priority

the objective is less tears,

more smiles soon happiness reappears,

state of depression is a terrible place,

we all deserve to have happiness on our face,

form a plan,

more smiles because is in your hand,

time is a precious thing to waste,

focus on having more smiles on your face.

~Let It Go~

Life circumstances can be unexplainable,
there are things out of our control,

Past pain only holds us back,

Grudges only drain us in the long run of life,
Future sets us free,
We hold on to the past,
and then we allow it to break us,

Look ahead never look backwards,
past pain cause insecurities,
Doubt cause us to question ourselves,

the past can either make us,
or can break us to a million pieces,
Forgiveness is the ultimate key,
let go of past hurt & pain.

~Alluring Intrigue~

You're a person worth having,

your voice is enchanting,

you keep family & friends laughing ,

Your spirit,

is presence & intuition is gifted,

No matter how much life takes its toll,

you remain pure in soul,

Personality rare & unmatchable,

you truly are valuable,

during chaos & trouble,

you relate to things in a way that is understandable,

Your to yourself,

maintain great health,

As an individual your caring,

unlike any other there is no comparing,

Steadily maturing,

your alluring,

during conversations your reassuring,

Rare & unique style,

the most beautiful smile,

No matter how much you stumble,

never will you tumble ,

only remain humble,

Others aren't even in your league,

a person like you has intrigue.

~Stepping Stone~

You won't know where to head,
if you don't know where you going,
as we grow into our own,
we got to maintain & pace ourselves,

Complacency is never good,
stepping stone is temporary,
progression is necessary,
success is on the individual,

A stepping stone doesn't mean dead end,
stepping stone means more to come,
more to conquer & overcome,
bigger challenges & obstacles to surpass,

Destiny is in our hands,
don't get discouraged,
bigger & brighter things are on the way.

~*Follow The Leader*~

Pave your own lane,

lead your own success train,

no pain , no gain,

travel at your own pace,

life is not a race,

no matter the adversity in your face,

don't give up on your chase,

till you reach your rightful place,

Let your destiny manifest,

continue to be the best,

Success is only fitting,

thou shall be no quitting,

Let the competition feel your wrath,

focus on your own path,

It's no telling how momentum can swing,

follow the leader & King.

Chapter Five

Astrology

~Aries~

Always in search of an experience that is epic,
the life of the party & fully energetic,

Takes care of responsibilities on a daily basis,
truly spontaneous,

Aries can be wild,
Aries live an active lifestyle,

Aries make things happen,
Aries are all about action,

Aries take measures that are drastic,
Always positive & enthusiastic,

Aries are rare & different,
fun loving & crave excitement,

Have tons of respect & dignity,
show signs of versatility,
filled with creativity,

At their worst their tempers may be explosive,

sometimes they can be impulsive,

Can be very competitive,

but their positive outweigh their negative,

Quick to offer feedback,

quick to react,

Aries are the leaders of the zodiac.

~Taurus~

One fact is undeniable,
Taurus are truly Reliable,

Taurus are very likable,
their personality is very desirable,

Taurus are good with making a strategy,
they live on practicality,

Taurus always want better & greater,
Taurus are independent in nature,

Taurus know how to build a strong foundation,
nobody matches Taurus when it comes to being
patient,

Taurus can be at times very distant,
but are very persistent,

Taurus are goal oriented,
thru life they follow their own method,

At their worst Taurus can be stuck in their ways,

often stubborn & going thru a lazy stage,

When Taurus has motivation,

they can accomplish anything with dedication,

Taurus are very dependable,

Taurus are incredible.

~Gemini~

Independent & clever,
Gemini is one of the best ever,
Nobody does it better,
Gemini is truly valuable,
Diverse & adaptable,
With Gemini anything is possible,
With Gemini nothing stays the same,
Gemini love freedom & change,
When it comes to Gemini,
They are a Social Butterfly,
Gemini is witty & fast,
Loves to multitask,
Loves good conversation,
Gemini has great observation,
Loves to learn new information,
Positive & optimistic,
Sadly Gemini can be materialistic,
One key weakness,
Gemini can be flirtatious,
Gemini is always curious,
Easy & out going,
Gemini is always dreaming & hoping,
One drawback of Gemini is inconsistency,
Gemini must have faith in their ability,
The uniqueness of this sign,
 Gemini is one of a kind.

~Cancer~

Emotional & loving,

cancer is remarkable & stunning,

Cancer is very ambitious ,

Always on top of business,

Cancer is helpful & compassionate,

motivated & talented

In relationships they are demanding,

but cancers are very understanding,

Cancers lives to be happy,

loves their friends & family,

Cancer is a romantic lover,

cancer is all about the structure,

cancer are well organized,

Cancer is a friend who is nurturing,

dependable & caring,

drawbacks of cancer is their bossy,

When depressed can be overly moody,

but cancers remain a thing of beauty,

Cancers are sophisticated,

cancers are very appreciated.

~Leo~

Leo's have high confidence,

Leo is powerful & dominant,

Leo's don't pass judgement,

Leo's demand respect,

Leo's are very honest & direct,

everything doesn't have to be perfect,

Leo's don't hold a grudge or anger,

Leo's is fun & full of laughter,

comes thru when it matter,

Leo love to lavish & extravagant,

Leo have knowledge & full of enlightenment,

Leo's are never nervous,

always adventurous,

drawback is Leo can be very egotistical,

tends to be vain & might try to belittle,

Leo won't run from any issue,

nothing can measure their value,

Leo overcome any & every struggle,

Leo is truly the king of the jungle.

~*Virgo*~

When comes to anything Virgo is flexible,

not arrogant but very humble,

Virgo's are naturally an introvert,

always on alert,

Virgo clever & intelligent since birth,

Virgo are down to earth,

They rather keep to themselves then socialize,

Virgo have tremendous ability to analyze,

Virgo love stability,

rarely do they show signs of vulnerability

At times can be judgmental,

practical & patience is essential,

Virgo's are very careful,

at their worst may tend to settle,

questioning things & always skeptical,

Although they may procrastinate,

they can hit or miss when it's time to communicate,

It's no debate,

Virgo is truly great.

~*Libra*~

No sign is more determined & ready,
gentle, sociable & friendly,
Libra is one of the best,
Libra is truly blessed,
Libra is clever & diplomatic,
Libra is never one to panic,
outgoing & exciting,
Libra is inspiring,
never down always self-motivated,
Libra is dedicated,
birthday during the season of autumn,
Libra hates being restricted & boredom,
love to party & fun loving,
at times Libra is inconsiderate,
Libra has more than one weakness,
at their best their fearless,
smart & well educated,
moves precise & well calculated,
if you got a Libra you got a keeper,
Libra is a natural leader.

~Scorpio~

The sign that is most intuitive,
but can be very sensitive,
Scorpio is very mysterious,
deep thinking & curious,
Scorpio feelings run deeply,
Scorpio act freely,
Scorpio delivers its caring sympathies,
Scorpio has tons of great qualities,
observant to details,
Scorpio rarely fails,
always on top & prevails,
compassionate & romantic,
behavior at its worst is erratic,
Scorpio can be charismatic,
Scorpio can be pessimistic,
stubborn & obsessive,
Scorpio is truly fascinating,
downright amazing,
Scorpio is epitome of captivating.

~Sagittarius~

Adventurer & risk taker,

not afraid of danger,

always in search of greater,

Sagittarius love freedom & love to explore,

always wanting to learn more,

Sagittarius is a sign of greatness,

with anything in life they are courageous,

very independent & spontaneous,

this sign is nowhere near laziness,

Sagittarius are very straightforward,

Sagittarius perform well under pressure,

Sagittarius is rare treasure,

At their worst they are reckless,

easily bored & easily jealous,

can be very careless,

although tactless & speaks bluntly,

Sagittarius shines confidently,

actions & words speak boldly,

Sagittarius is marvelous,

one word to describe this sign is fabulous.

~Capricorn~

Capricorn are practical & follow the basics,
Capricorn are workaholics,
Capricorn love structure & organization,
success is the ultimate gratification,
Capricorn wants stability,
takes things in their own hands,
loves to make plans,
Capricorn won't stop till the task completed,
Capricorn can be very conceited,
Capricorn bossy personality is unnecessary,
first only, they hate being secondary,
cautious & always on guard,
Capricorn works extremely hard,
finishes everything they start,
kind, patient & very smart,
Capricorn doesn't seek validation,
at their worst they full of procrastination,
Capricorn has a tough time being committed,
often possessive & conceited,
can be pessimistic,
dispute the struggle they remain realistic,
no matter what part they choose,
Capricorn will not lose.

~Aquarius~

One sign that is unstoppable,
makes the impossible more possible,
truly brave & logical,
Aquarius can overcome any obstacle,
Aquarius is truly remarkable,
Aquarius is very inventive,
Aquarius is simply impressive,
quick to act so their impulsive,
exciting & definitely original,
having an Aquarius in your life is pivotal,
unpredictable you'll never know what they thinking,
Aquarius love dreaming & partying,
Aquarius love new things & variety,
Aquarius can be aloof from society,
Aquarius live life rightfully,
passionate in their ways,
often flirtatious,
can be very rebellious,
Aquarius is precious,
at times can be sweet & innocent,
Aquarius is magnificent.

~Pisces~

Pisces are masters of loyalty,

being sympathetic is their specialty,

Pisces move thru life carefully,

their personality is so heavenly

Pisces feel a deep sense of empathy,

very caring & very accepting,

true masters of nurturing

a natural introverted soul,

seeing others happy makes Pisces whole,

loving people & extremely sensitive,

never are they negative,

Pisces personality is irresistible

Pisces are very spiritual,

often unpredictable

at their worst they are moody & indecisive,

doesn't like people & very reclusive,

hard to pin down & very elusive,

Pisces live in their mind,

Pisces is the most enchanted zodiac sign,

Pisces is deeply emotional

Pisces is exceptional.

Chapter Six

Sex + Intimacy +Passion

~10 Commandments of Pleasure~

Number one,

thou shall be spontaneous,

thou shall pleasure beyond the wildest limits,

sex in the craziest places,

Number two,

thou shall make fantasies come true,

Number three,

seduce your mate mentally,

double dose of love & stimulation,

make love to the soul,

Number four,

versatility is necessary,

switch it up nightly,

spice it up monthly,

Number five,

be both naughty & nice,

make love on Monday,

sex like porn stars on Tuesday,

be gentle & sensual during the day,

be aggressive during the night,

mix & match with your loving,

Number six,

make it nasty,

don't hold back on sexual urges,

turn your bedroom into a jungle,

Number seven,

anything goes in the bedroom,

ice melting on skin,

whip cream all over the body,

chocolate mixed in,

Number eight,

hit play & record,

create your own lasting movie,

let the passion flow,

lights camera Action,

Number nine,

use each second to make a lasting impression,

Number ten,

satisfaction is top priority,

happiness is a must,

pleasuring you is honor that I cherish forever.

~*The Seduction of Victoria*~

It's Honeymoon night in Paris France,
tonight is my chance,
to give my wife Victoria Bell-Wesley the ultimate
romance,
My enchanted Pisces queen,
as we arrive on the scene,
I hold ya hand, & I promise tonight will be grand,
Hot Sex & orgasms is the plan,
The 5 star resort is the venue,
and your body is on the menu,
may I continue,
I go from hard to gentle to light,
dear wife I'm going do you right,
I'm your knocking boots & ringing your Bell
tonight,
First it's dinner then it's romance time,
tonight your mine,
Let our intense passion soar,
feel the stroke of this lion roar,
from the bed to the kitchen to the floor,
and yet you still want more,
After dinner we head back to the room,
where our passion will bloom,
Soft sheets & warm covers,
perfect setting for Lovers,

Undress you head to toe,
nice & slow,
Kiss your neck & rip off your bra,
I look in amazement & awe,
Kiss & lick your breast,
your pants & panties come off next,
As I kiss my way down to your hips,
the bed sheets you tightly grip,
as my tongue intertwines with your pussy lips,
The right mix of pleasure & pain,
this whole resort going know my name,
As I stroke you senseless,
you get breathless,
Plant your feet on my shoulder,
your G-Spot stimulated as I pull you closer,
Pussy sweet as an arrangement that's edible,
switching new positions got you turning flexible,
it's amazing how we connect emotional,
blend sexual & spiritual,
Hands down your body feel my sensual touch,
heart pounding fast you feeling that adrenaline
rush,
Mind blowing,
pussy soaking,
me on top as I'm deep stroking,
you on the bottom lip biting & moaning,
You busting orgasms & sweat,

your pussy getting more wet,
Pisces & Leo sexual addiction,
We switch multiple positions,
you get wild & release your inhibitions,
your pleasure is tonight's mission,
I'm your best friend, husband & your sexual maniac,
tonight was no mistake,
your romance bliss as your legs shake,
Tonight was our love making soundtrack,
ending with pleasurable climax,
As we cuddle,
as a couple,
Here is gift of a diamond necklace for you,
to show you my love & our marriage is true,
It's amazing how our love grew,
just wait here comes seduction of Victoria part 2.

~In Love with A Married Woman~

This affair feel so wrong,
but the sex is so passionately strong,
Dispute you having a wedding ring,
we still have a romantic fling,
but this is more than just a sex thing,
I hate our goodbyes & farewells,
I love our getaways at nice hotels,
I love the time we spend,
no longer can I pretend,
I'm in love with a married lady,
that I love greatly,
call me crazy,
but this feeling is scary,
Even more crazy is that you have a family,
but your truly unhappy,
The marriage is a disaster,
now you want to leave for greater pastures,
I may not have all the answers,
but I know your happiness matters,

In a relationship you should never feel alone,

we shouldn't fear the unknown,

abuse we shouldn't condone,

black eyes & broken bone,

true passion makes you moan,

true love makes happy to come home,

For his behavior there is no excuse,

only in the bedroom will I seduce,

let's put our great qualities to use,

Together we are a powerful force,

I'll patiently wait for you to get a divorce,

then let our passion run its course,

This love will no longer be forbidden,

we both are love bitten,

it's no need to keep this hidden,

great sex every night while I'm pulling out your weave,

your stresses I will relieve,

I got much more planned for later,

all you have to do is sign on the divorce paper,

Let's start our own family or raise a baby,

I can't help that I'm in love with a married lady.

~Sex Is Beautiful~

Sex has been around since the dawn of time,

people of all ages sex every day & every week,

We all enjoy sex in a variety of ways,

we act on attraction but we can't control who we

have feelings for,

We should never feel ashamed for our fantasies,

sex at its best is healthy,

sex at worst can be downright deadly,

There is no such thing as too much sex,

nothing better erases your stress,

Nothing is more beautiful than two souls

intertwining,

passion is beautiful amongst two people,

There is no better ending then the perfect climax,

sex isn't complex

Sex is lovely & thrilling

sex clinches the soul,

sex is beautiful.

~Stroke of Genius~

As each stroke gets deeper,

you go from moaner to screamer,

This feeling is intoxicating,

this stroke is so dominating,

I know you been long awaiting,

better yet anticipating,

your mind & body both stimulating,

As I stroke it to the right,

I'll make your night,

Stroke it to the left direction,

you feel in heaven,

Quick fast & in slow motion,

but you wetter than the ocean,

maybe it's my stroke that tingles your emotion,

unleashes your orgasmic explosion,

Nothing will be the same,

my stroke drives you insane,

the right mix of pleasure & pain,

no wonder the neighborhood knows my name,

My stroke cuts you no slack,

keeps you coming back,

I love how you react,
This stroke is fearless,
I know it's your weakness,
the stroke of genius.

~Side Chick Fever~

When did it become acceptable play second place,
to play a side piece & be perfectly content,
to be loyal to an unloyal person,
Why did our self-esteem sink below new levels,
chicks bragging about having someone else man,
throwing slick shots thru social media every day,
What's so great about being a home wrecker,
side chicks are exploiting a weakness in the
relationship,
A lot of homes aren't happy as they seem,
that allows the side chick to take advantage,
A lot of people want their cake & eat it too,
people always think the grass is greener on the other
side,
Some just want what they can't have,
selfish individuals just need to stay single,
A side chick is just in it for her own gain,
side chicks nowadays even overstep their
boundaries,
Sides chicks want quality time,
side chicks want PDA,

side chicks are striving to be main chicks,

but often it's the cheating guy who allows all of this,

A lot of ladies are happy & proud to be on the
sidelines,

This problem faces many relationships,

but this can be dodged,

it all starts with standards & trust,

The main lady needs to stand by her standards,

don't settle for anything less than your happiness,

But as a strong woman it's hard to focus,

when it's someone ready to take your spot,

there is always someone waiting on the sidelines.

~*Promiscuous Stage*~

A stage that is often risky,

a stage where lots of men & women get busy,

Sex drive runs rampant,

standards & morals go absent,

we make a bad judgement,

poor choices & bad life management,

devastating effects could be permanent,

sexual conquests often turbulent,

Sex partners builds notches on some guys belts,

all this sex is hazardous to health,

Especially if you don't use protection,

sex won't always be perfection,

some are just misguided & need direction,

Dispute all the sex & anger,

sex to disguise how you feel isn't the answer,

life can be a tease,

promiscuous people aim to please,

be careful not to catch a disease,

During this stage people behave stupidly,

act immature & foolishly,

so much raw sex & nudity,

All because of promiscuity,
sex is about love & unity,
making love oh so beautifully,
Promiscuity leads down a bad path,
where people ridicule & laugh,
but they don't know the half,
Only you know your story,
after this stage of you being horny,
then comes the happiness & glory,
For some it means coming of age,
a lot of people go thru a promiscuous stage.

~*Blue Velvet Room*~

Welcome to my sanctuary,

where the sex is heavy,

The pleasure is everlasting ,

never at a loss for passion,

Between the vanilla & blueberries,

the level of sex & foreplay varies,

No rules,

lots of toys & tools,

It all goes down in the blue velvet room,

where fantasies loom,

where the sex is hotter the summer month of June,

sex during the full moon,

sex in your craziest costume,

It's no telling what you'll step into,

or crazy sex that will ensue,

in this room that is blue,

the priorities are climax & pleasuring you,

when that blue light comes on that's the cue,

what freaky things will you do,

The curious mind wonders,

what craziness will happen under the covers,

Don't be modest,

sex at your hardest,

be honest,

deliver on the sexual deeds you promised,

Be single for tonight,

go on a sexual flight,

let your wildest desires bloom,

it all goes down in the blue velvet room.

~Temptation & Desire~

Temptation is crazy in a sexual way,
desire is in all of us,
forbidden fruit tempts us all,
desire is uncontrollable,

Temptation creates lust,
desire creates intrigue,
temptation is hard to resist,
desire is hard to ignore,

Temptation creates butterflies,
desire is pleasing to the eye,
temptation makes you play with fire,
desire makes you want to act,

Temptation makes you think,
desire makes hesitate,
temptation is worth the risk,
desire makes you question,

Both feelings have a deep impact,
both feelings take on a life of their own,
both feelings are hard to ignore,
both feelings play tricks on our mind.

~BaeCation~

I got champagne bottles to uncork

Let's Sex in New York,

Make Love in Manhattan,

go on multiple shopping transactions,

Let's make magic happen,

maybe rent a cabin,

check out stores & the latest fashion,

I got better plans

let's go see a football game at the meadowlands,

Let's hold hands,

kiss in the stands,

What will it be tomorrow,

maybe a night in buffalo,

Christmas time we kiss under a mistletoe,

During this trip we make love & witness history,

let's check out the Statue of Liberty

Let's be romantic in a new area,

let's get nasty in Philadelphia,

Stroke you till your leg shake,

then take a break,

then get a Philadelphia cheese steak,

Doesn't matter if it's Connecticut

I'll remain affectionate

if we in Boston I'll be compassionate,

in Washington I'll be nice & dedicate,

no matter the city on the east coast,

I'll love you the most,

But we got new sights to see,

this is a trip you'll love I guarantee,

to the south we go for part 2,

a Baecation between me & you.

~Baecation II~

Where will bow down on one knee,

maybe in Tennessee,

from Knoxville to Nashville,

in romantic suite we will chill,

with lots of time to kill,

tonight will be a thrill,

something passionate you can feel,

in Memphis we eat a delicious meal,

Travel to Dallas,

treat you like a leading actress,

make love from the shower to the mattress,

Then travel to Houston were we will have a problem,

I'll give you multiple orgasms often,

Then it's on in San Antonio,

where you can ride me like a rodeo,

you be my Juliet I'll be Romeo,

hot sex on the patio,

blushing with an afterglow,

let our love overflow,

Then it's onto Atlanta where the fun don't stop,

where I make your panties wet then drop,

then we shop,

Living it up in Atlanta,

now it's on to Tampa,

where we check out the scene,

Introduce you as my queen,

then travel to Miami,

Where we will marry,

then live happy,

No matter the location,

we will make it our Baecation,

~Red Silk Panties~

You always make my mind wonder,

something about those red panties that make stop &

stutter,

let's sex on top of the cover,

It's words I can't even explain,

those red silk panties drive me insane,

You got the red lingerie to match,

you're the perfect catch,

You know I love you in red,

the way your legs spread,

the way you lay in the bed,

Purely made out of silk,

but you taste like finest milk,

I'll buy them for you as much as needed,

red silk panties from Victoria secret,

I won't stop satisfying you till the job is completed

With your waist thin,

you unleash the beast within,

with the way the red silk panties hug your skin,

Put on those panties for daddy,

red silk panties make me happy.

~A Woman Named Ashley~

It was a warm summer night,
a woman named Ashley was looking oh so right,
We were at a movie,
she is & forever will be a beauty,
It was a movie about a zombie apocalypse,
my mind was on her enchanting eyes & kissable lips,
Truly unlike any other,
truly a beauty that makes your mind wonder,
She is more than imagination,
she is smart & full of determination,
Looking sexy while wearing a black dress,
looking like the definition of excellence & success,
but I must confess,
Ashley had my mind racing,
tonight could be life changing,
we could go from dating to love making,
Or it could be just us catching a flick,
Ashley wasn't your average chick,
Gemini soul & spirit,
tonight I want to take things to a new limit,
Our hands starting moving,
we no longer cared about the movie we was viewing,

Hot sex & many orgasms was brewing,
in the theaters we kissing & touching,
Touching on me I was rock hard,
but she wasn't caught off guard,
Her eyes closed as I was rubbing,
she was soak & wet she was flooding,
soon as the movie ended we was rushing,
I was excited & she was blushing,
To the car we went running,
we both knew tonight was going to be truly
something,
Soon as the car doors close,
passion arose,
We couldn't keep our hands off each other,
tonight we will define our summer,
I say " your place or mine"
she says" Anywhere is fine"
I was thinking the backseat,
but Ashley is special & deserves to be romanced
on soft cover sheets,
we decided on a nice hotel with a romantic suite,
a great woman deserves something sweet,
Soon as we got in the room,
it was she was a bride & I was a groom,
hot passionate sex was about to bloom,
I carried her to the bed,
undressed her then soon her legs spread,

I licked her from head to toe,
I knew she loved it hot but nice & slow,
Kisses to her inner thigh,
I could see the enjoyment in her eye,
This area became my playground,
my tongue knows no limit or bound,
I licked my way up to her breast,
she was impressed,
Kissing on her neck made her lose control,
climax & satisfaction of her needs was my goal,
I soon put her legs on my shoulders & stroke her
to a beautiful rhythm,
this bedroom was my kingdom,
Moans & groans,
as I kiss & stroke her erotic zones,
Lust plus passion I feel her getting more wet,
we going multiple rounds without busting a
sweat,
No time to relax,
I look her in her eyes as we both climax,
we cuddle,
I promise to rid her of any struggle,
rid her of any stress & trouble,
We kiss,
forever promise one another passionate bliss,
We truly made each other happy,
thank god for a woman named Ashley.

~*Great Sexpectations*~

Sex comes with many temptations,

but also follows many expectations,

views on sex change over the generations,

Somethings we desire,

others we don't need or require,

You can be more then able,

but you'll still have a label,

You either nasty or basic,

you either modern or classic,

Sex can be full of magic,

sex can also be tragic,

You can dry or overly dramatic,

unemotional or downright romantic,

Whether your sexual experience is traumatic,

everlasting & fantastic,

It's the experience that matters,

enjoyment is based on a lot of factors,

it's life itself that gives us many answers,

With sex comes pressure,

it's not always about pleasure,

sex gives us a lifetime of pain nobody can measure,

sex is without error,

With sex you got to proceed with caution & safety,

strap up to prevent diseases & baby,

Life is crazy,

sex can be scary,

If you sexually active weekly or daily,

try to get tested regularly,

your health is the gift of luxury,

have sex with someone worthy,

don't rush to be in a hurry

Take your time,

enjoy the youth that is your prime,

Be clear & honest,

tomorrow isn't promised,

No matter the expectation do your part,

Cherish life & play it smart.

~Best Climax Ever~

The best is yet to come,
the best sex leaves a woman legs numb,
bang like the rhythm of a drum,
every lady knows where their best came from,

Heavy breathing with the heart racing,
eyes gazing,
temperatures raising, legs shaking,
climax that is simply amazing,

Heavy sweat & bed breaking,
heavy kissing & love making,
lust & erotic behavior,
pure passion waking up thy neighbor,

With the best climax there is no contest
fulfilling the climax & conquest,
the true difference with the best,
it separates itself from the rest

Climax is relaxing feeling,
climax the ultimate healing,
nothing beats the best climax,
that's a well-known fact.

Chapter Seven

Millennial Renaissance

~Justice & Prosecution~

There is no such thing as sinners,

likewise for saints,

We all are individuals that are capable of both good &

bad,

some of us are just trying do right with limited

mistakes,

While the rest hardly ever know right is,

but sometimes bad things happen,

Things go from worse to horrible,

we live in a world,

Where we are judged by our past,

our future gets measured & over analyzed by

potential,

People judge a book by its cover,

without even reading a single letter,

Pretend to know your story without reading a single

page,

people want be crucify you under any situation,

Make you out to be guilty without your side of the

story,

our mistakes get held against us forever,

Guilty until proven innocent or just plain guilty,

instead of a jury of our peers,

We prosecuted to the fullest degree,

people want to play Judge & jury,

Give your life sentence of judgement,

in life we get judged daily,

We rise & we fall,

thou shall not hold your head down in shame,

God has your back thru it all,

one person can rise above a jury,

one person can rise above a judge,

No matter how much they talk or criticize,

only God can judge you.

~Revisionist~

Life is full of many experiences,
some experiences can be good & bad,
Lessons may be hard,
we either get better or worse,
Decisions can be rough,
we can't shed a tear about what's behind us,
always look ahead to what's in front of you,
We can't go back & change the past,
we live & cherish the now,
We can't go back & modify an previous event,
moving forward we find answers,
moving back all we get is lessons,
We can't change the past because of how we view it
today,
we got to accept what is & what is not,
Let the past be what it was,
not for what we want it to be,
History can't be changed,
future is what you make it,
Anything is possible,
fool me once shame on you,
fool me twice & I never learned the first time,
Past can't be redone or revised,
history may repeat,
Present is to be loved & appreciated,
today is gift make each moment count for your
happiness.

~*Materialistic Society*~

People these days are too obsessed with brands,
instead making life goals & plans,
life has many demands,
Shiny cars,
people idolizing celebrity superstars,
Fancy jewelry,
but as a community,
Where is unity,
materialistic chances we seize to pass up the
opportunity,
as a society,
where is our dignity,
Brand new expensive shoes,
but stagnant lifestyle & don't mix with ignorant
views,
God in your life you can't lose,
Some people have champagne taste,
but a mind is a terrible thing to waste,
Some people like to stunt,
others like to front,
Money doesn't always bring happiness,
sometimes it bring sadness,
Happiness doesn't involve status,
big houses or a huge palace,
Pocket full of money but your life full of malice,
people chasing diamonds & gold,
being overly materialistic gets old,

Young kids aren't focused on being a doctor,
not focused on getting smarter,
Society focused on the almighty dollar,
but if money makes you scream or holler,
Then your soul is poor & weak,
it's about the quality that is truly unique,
Your taste shouldn't be expensive,
money shouldn't be your prime motive,
If money is your idea of being realistic,
then you are simply materialistic.

~Playing Keep Up~

Life at times feels like a race,

with people fighting for first place,

we spend our entire lives trying to keep up the pace,

sometimes to help our self-esteem other times to save face,

but whatever is the case,

Life is about striving,

happiness & thriving,

things in life are a matter of timing,

no matter the mountain of obstacles your climbing,

or the tough path you're driving,

life is about surviving,

with the end result leaving you smiling,

Think ahead,

don't listen to words said,

Don't pay attention to the trends people follow,

be yourself is always the motto,

When it comes to life we are always in a hurry,

never too late never too early,

We feel like we should our life together,

it's life & our peers that cause the pressure,

goal is to make your life better,

When it comes to our life we often are too critical,

nit picking & overly analytical,

We feel pressured to perfect,

feeling like things should be correct,

We got to learn to let life play out,

have no doubt,

stand tall & proud,

don't try to keep up with the crowd,

Life isn't about luck,

when you a leader you don't have to keep up.

~The Decline of Privacy~

With technology comes a new emergence,

somethings cause a huge disturbance,

privacy is a huge impotence ,

Seems live our privacy is shrinking,

what is society thinking,

We now have chips in our MasterCard & our visa,

we stay on social media,

Privacy is a problem in the nation,

way too much privacy invasion,

Not enough respect,

but with fame & popularity what do we expect,

People love to be up close,

to get a triple dose,

Of your business,

just so they can be nosy & witness,

Whether it's on Instagram, Twitter or Facebook,

people are always going to take an extra look,

Maybe even a sneak peak,

paying close attention to you every day of the week,

with music we steady searching for latest leak,

When did our privacy drop,

when will the madness stop,

When did technology get this advance,

we got to take a stance,

or it will be anything goes,

then who knows,

Here is what I propose,

keep all personal info,

on the low,

Keep it protected,

when it comes to your privacy you got to be

invested,

Privacy may be shrinking every day,

with social media & hackers here to stay,

it's important you remain protected in every way.

As it currently stands,

privacy is in your hands.

~Hard Pill To Swallow~

Truth sets you free,

truth hurts in any circumstance,

truth cleanses the soul,

truth frees the mind to many possibilities,

A lot of people can't lie to save their lives,

some lie because it's in their nature,

A lie don't care who tell it,

half & half makes no difference,

truth may come easy for some,

While others it may be nonexistent,

truth can be a reality check for some,

A dose of reality can put people in check,

a rare breed of individual fear truth,

Truth brings clarity,

truth brings pain,

truth brings forth circumstances we can't expect,

A lie people can handle,

a lie can balance expectations,

a lie keeps people at ease,

truth is the ultimate antidote,

truth is a tough pill to swallow.

~Selfie Generation~

Nowadays everybody strikes a pose for a camera,
our smartphones are sophisticated cameras in
themselves,
with a push of a button,
you get an instant snap or many snaps,
From one filter to many filters,
a picture is worth a thousand words,
a picture can be full of deceptions,
But yet we are so obsessed with selfies,
we analyze profile pictures,
create catchy captions,
go thru multiple filters,
All for the end result of looking good,
or appearing to look good for others,
while dating we beg for everyone to "Send Me A
Picture "
We double tap for a " Like" ,
but ignore it if we don't like it,
We give it a thumbs up for support,
or thumbs down for a dislike,
People will do anything for a like,
taking selfies has seriously become an addiction,
Nothing wrong with taking pics,
but when it over consume your life & everything in it,
then it becomes a serious problem,
People take themselves too serious these days,
generation spoiled with self,

is it any wonder why we so selfish,
Nothing wrong with love of self,
understand a picture doesn't say much,
understand a picture only tells half the story,
but a picture is worth a thousand words.

~Divorce Effect~

There is no debating,
the effects of divorce can be devastating,
with pressure & problems escalating
Arguments out of control,
families being incomplete & not whole,
Divorce for a family is major,
nowadays married couples are quick to sign divorce paper,
Married couples that have lasted should be saluted,
things break marriages apart nowadays are stupid,
So many things are destroying the family unit,
infidelity is definitely included,
Problems can be fixed no matter how small,
United we stand divided we fall,
Separates sister from brother,
effects how kids look at each other,
makes kids mind wonder,
Soon the kids start placing blame,
to mask the pain,
Single parent Household nobody knows the struggle & strain,
how it leaves you physically & emotionally drain,
How it effects the kids childhood,
shapes their views into adulthood,
No marriage is perfect,
but divorce has a devastating effect.

~90's Kid~

Memories are everlasting,
90's left an Imprint on all of us,

Before text messages we passed folded notes,
before social media we did 3 way phone
conversations,

Hi top fades & Nike kicks,
Cartoons & TV Shows galore,

From bugs bunny to home improvement,
from Martin to Fresh Prince of Bel Air,

Kids playing with water guns & playing Hide & seek,
teens watching Saturday nickelodeon & dreaming of
being slimed,

Goosebumps was in every kid possession,
a time when everyone was in love with wresting
whether it was WWF or WCW,

A time where overalls & Tommy Hilfiger was in style,
a time where pagers were the hottest thing around,

Music was the best & the artists were classic,
a time were recording your favorite song off the radio
onto a tape was masterful,

Your favorite basketball players were either Michael
Jordan, Grant Hill or Shaq,
your favorite hip hop artists were either 2pac,
Notorious BIG or Snoop Doggy Dogg,

A time were TV guide was your best friend,
a time full of VHS tapes & blockbuster,

A time where everybody wanted to be a power
ranger,
Disney movies leaving us with joy & tears at the
same time,

Our president was Bill Clinton,
a time where kids actually played outside,

a time where MTV showed videos nonstop,

A Great Time to be a Kid,
A Great Time to be Alive.

~Marijuana Legalization~

As time progresses & changes,
so does our mind & thinking,
we were watch ignorant,
Now we are educated & well informed,
we focus so much drug prevention,
not enough on overdose & awareness,
with legalization court costs & crime will drop,
While jobs & resources will increase,
government will greatly benefit from tax revenue,
Marijuana needs to be treated the same as Alcohol &
tobacco products,
Consequences are far greater with alcohol then
anything,
Marijuana at minimum use is recreational,
more then 45% of people use marijuana,
Support has increased over the years for legalization,
medical use has strong support,
Decriminalizing marijuana has large support from
everyone,
Drug charges are outrageously unbalanced
compared to other crimes,

due to more awareness & effects coming to light,

society places unfair judgment on things it doesn't
understand,

But let's anything slide long as they can tax it &
monetize it,

society can be contradicting,

we can't allow society to shape our every viewpoint,

We must educate & inform ourselves,

since 2012 many places have legalized marijuana,

As time goes on many more states will join in the act,

finally a step in the right direction,

change is always positive,

times are now changing for the better.

~No Tolerance~

Violence isn't the answer,
we must learn to control our temper & anger,
Learn to get to the heart of the matter,
our tolerance is something we got to maintain &
master,
before the wrong action leads to disaster,
verbal abuse is one contributing factor,
Words said leave a devastating effect,
we all aren't perfect,
we all got issues to correct,
speak highly never indirect,
Be honest & never shoot a subliminal,
abusive people are highly egotistical,
always being judgmental,
my way or the highway violent & hypocritical,
but that's no excuse to get physical,
Thou shall not assault,
we must find solutions not find fault,
why abuse your one true soulmate,
We need more love & less hate,
thou shall not be blind,
to any neglect or abuse of any kind,
Fellas keep your hands in check,
have respect,
Any lady that you got to hit,
is a woman you don't need to be with,
no matter how much you get upset,

never make a death threat,
you wouldn't want to do something you'll regret,
Abuse can be prevented,
if worst come to worst then you can always exit,
Violence & a use is something we have to reduce,
dear ladies no love is worth enduring violence,
leaving you with black eyes or in an ambulance,
pay attention to any red flags as signs or evidence,
Do not provoke or strike a blow,
if worst come to worst then hit then door & go,
Your health & well-being is what you protect & save,
rather than be sorry of buried in a grave,
we as people got to learn to behave,
We should always cherish life & ourselves,
thou shall keep thy hands to themselves.

~Turn Up Life~

Living life on the edge can be fun,
but falling off the edge is costly,
we get so consumed with excitement,
we lose ourselves in the process,
We want this moment for life,
till we can't the consequences that come with it,
We living strictly for the "Turn Up"
when we really need to get our priorities up,
we rather be high or highly intoxicated,
We hate being sober,
recreational habits become overdosing,
We lose sense of ourselves,
goals no longer are pursued,
Our support system breaks down,
priorities become non important,
Nothing is wrong with having fun,
it just comes down to balance,
Turn up life causes many regrets,
turn up life causes us to lose perspective,
turn up life is nothing more than a phase,
but it can be maintained,

with good family friends you'll never feel worthless,

Some people are only around to turn up with you,

a lot of people are around for turn up & success,

But where are they when there is struggle,

your real support system is there no matter the circumstances,

Turn up life leads to perfect attendance at the club,

turn up life will have you experimenting with all kinds of drugs,

We must find the balance in ourselves & our life,

Because life is more than just a turn up,

life is beautiful.

~Benefits of Having a Homeboy~

Some people come & go,

some bonds progress & grow,

some are loyal & some only pretend,

Men & women can be cool as friends

this a relationship not everyone comprehends,

There things & feelings to be disputed,

but it can be concluded,

a relationship of this kind has benefits included,

Friends of the opposite sex,

are always the best,

They instill knowledge,

provide you with a positive message,

Give your insight & feedback,

help you in the areas you lack,

Teach you what to do & not do,

thru it all remaining true,

Homeboys can help separate the bad apples from the bunch,

separate the winner from the chump,

Separate the ones who serious from the one who
playing games,
listen as your homeboy carefully explains,
as he teaches you how to dodge the lames,
We as men & women both experience growing pain,
with a relationship like this it's a lot to gain,
It's great when both sexes treat each other as equal,
respect one another as people,
benefits of having a homeboy are truly beneficial,
Nobody deserves to be played with like a toy,
great things happen when you have benefits of
having a homeboy.

~Netflix & Chill~

What's up with dating in this generation,

love & romance is the happiest declaration,

with dating where is effort & appreciation,

Where is flattery & compliments,

where are the heartfelt moments,

Not everything has to be romantic,

not every action has to be drastic,

but every woman deserves to feel fantastic,

Dating is about finding a spark or creating magic,

it seems like dating is in a state of panic,

Nights on the town,

have turned into condoms, sex & lounging around,

We looking too hard to poke & stroke,

no more night outs just drink & smoke,

you can still date if you broke,

Just comes down to being creative,

putting your best foot forward with good intent &
motive,

Nowadays it's chilling & Netflix,

most guys are doing this with a lot of chicks,

not knocking the Netflix & chill technique,

but understand every woman is unique,

Ladies don't let your standards be weak,

fellas be consistent & mean every word you speak,

take your effort & romance to a higher peak,

As a potential boyfriend you have a position to fill,

loving a woman takes passion & skill,

a great woman deserves more than Netflix & chill,

The art of romance I'm here to preserve,

give her the romance & love she deserve.

Chapter Eight

Classic Remastered

~As I Grow Wiser~

As I grow stronger & wiser,
I had almost lost my path,
but it was right then & there,
right in front of me,
Here I am,
one man army with determination,
with one goal & one dream,
But standing in my way,
is a road of obstacles,
some small others large as can be,
As I move forward,
obstacle get more in the way,
no obstacles shall detour my route,
because my final destination is the finish line,
I am a powerful black man,
motivated by goals & a powerful plan,
no obstacles shall interfere,
thou shall not give up,
As I grow stronger nothing will weigh heavy on my soul,
As I grow wiser I will overcome small talk & petty people,
what it takes to accomplish my goals,
what it takes to overcome any obstacles,
is my strength & resilience,
I'll accomplish my goals as I grow wiser.

~World Stage~

Life in itself is a stage,
some are tragic in nature while others are coming
of age,
Life has good guys & bad,
life has moments that leave you happy & mad,
makes you jump for joy or makes you cry &
makes you sad,
Life has characters who are full of personality,
life can instantly change dramatically,
Life may not always play out in your favor,
but you should progress & move forward with
humble behavior,
Iin life you have heroes & villains,
in life we have separate journeys & missions,
guided by ambitions,
from childhood to adulthood life is full of
transitions,
We start off as children wanting to learn,
one day at a time happily awaiting our turn,
Then we progress over life until we are a teenage,
causing pure chaos & rampage,
Progressing with strong maturity,
molded by life & puberty,
Life isn't about who the fastest & who late or
early,
it's no need to worry,
life is all about the journey,

It's about people playing their part,
they make grand entrances or slowly depart,
Some come around for a reason,
some barely lasted a season,
We all may be different & on a separate page
the world is clearly a stage.

~Word To The Wives~

You also have dreams,

your more than a wife,

you deserve a life,

Marriage is a union of two,

your freedom should never disappear,

life doesn't revolve around your husband,

Life includes him & your happiness,

never place your happiness on hold,

never fake your smile ever,

Be guided & be smart,

never dumb down,

whatever you want to be try to be great at it,

Never should your happiness not matter,

never should you settle for less,

Best thing in life is life itself,

cherish yourself ,

Cherish love ones,

consider this more than a word,

consider this a positive declaration,

Always be yourself,

remember you deserve to be happy too.

~*Guardian Angel*~

Guardian Angel helps you when you're in trouble,

guardian Angel won't let you stumble,

Your Angel will catch you with open arms,

no need to be alarm,

guardian Angel keeps you from harm,

Guardian Angel guides your decision making

process,

guardian Angel helps you make progress,

Never any step backwards,

helps you maintain your standards,

keeps you from dangerous hazards,

life is about moving upwards

Guardian Angel keeps you from making mistakes,

your guardian Angel knows what it takes,

guardian Angel keeps you away from the fakes & the

people who are snakes,

Guardian Angel will be the first to react,

guardian Angel will always have your back.

~Phenomenon Woman 2~

Gorgeous woman where does my beauty reside,
where does the confidence come with this stride,
as a woman maybe it comes from the inside,
the beauty within is something no woman should
hide,
with lord almighty as your guide,
it isn't no secret or lie,
that you as a phenomenal woman will survive,

The allure of your smile,
the way you phenomenally rock any & every
hairstyle,
A time with a phenomenal woman is truly worthwhile,
A phenomenal woman time is not to be wasted,
A phenomenal woman is one who is sacred,
A phenomenal woman can walk into any room with
captivation,
it takes a strong man to rule a nation,
but best believe a phenomenal woman is always a
part of the equation,

Phenomenal woman is one you marry & carry to the
alter,
words as soothing & organized as an author,
the only thing left for a phenomenal woman is to walk
on water,
a phenomenal woman always gets better & stronger,

Being a phenomenal woman isn't about piercings of
your nose & cheek,
it's more than having eyebrows on fleek,
Being phenomenal is not for the weak,
it's not about the cost of your bag,
it's not based on your swag,
it's not about the materialistic things that cause you
to brag,
it's about being yourself thru it all,
it's about rising when you fall
it's about having a living soul,
it's about betterment & accomplishing your goal,
Being all that you can be,
remaining true to self & being free,
standards maintained,
home trained,
phenomenal woman can't be contained
A phenomenal woman with more to offer then a
pretty face,
A phenomenal woman is one who can't be replaced,

~*Nightly Review*~

As the day concludes,
what a day full of infectious moods,
I had a day that fully includes,

Depression from life rejection,
bad luck was today's impression,
sadness was my facial expression,

Mondays often drag & suck,
long days can be tricky with bad luck,
stagnation will have you feeling stuck,

Say a prayer before rest,
as time goes so does the stress,
life is similar to a game of chess,

Our spirit can determine our fate,
resilience is a positive trait,
time is now for us to be great,

Thru all the trouble & malice,

thru all the chaos & madness,

life is a peaceful palace full of happiness,

In conclusion,

life can be full of confusion,

but keeping God first is the solution,

Even if the day was odd,

I shall always remain positive & thank god.

~*Dreams Vs Reality*~

In my dreams,

our love flows as a water stream,

As I lay a delicate kiss upon your cheek,

our attraction doesn't seem bleak,

I acknowledge you as my wife,

the one I cherish all my life,

Our vows are sacred,

look at the love we created,

Passion at its highest,

this love is truly the greatest,

Our passion is never ending,

best day of our life was our wedding,

I played my cards smart,

until death do us part,

When it comes to reality,

our relationship is crappy,

you can't stand the sight of me,

You wish I didn't exist,

my actions get dismissed,

the more I try & insist,

the more you deny & resist,

Dispute my grand appearance,

you still have your suspicions,

your my ultimate addiction,

But you was there was a cure,

you label my actions immature,

No matter my persistence,

you keep your distance,

your happiness comes with my disappearance,

it's not a goodbye it's good riddance,

Is this a fantasy or is it happening in actuality,

or is it just my dreams vs reality.

~Lonesome Mindset~

What a terrible mindset to have,

where you rather be sad then laugh,

when it come to the struggle we don't know the half,

Joy beats being bitter,

triumph beats being a quitter,

sadness is a heart colder then winter,

happiness is a depression killer,

It's better to be honest & open,

it's better to be fulfilled then broken,

lonely people deserve devotion,

full of love & emotion,

feeling appreciated beats being lonesome,

Loneliness leads to destruction,

a helping hand can make us function

With love of self you can achieve,

love of self is all you need,

please believe.

~*Powerful Voice*~

I heard a voice unlike any other,
it made my mind wonder,
It sounded so soulful & epic,
so much more then angelic,
So magical & timeless,
so wonderful & priceless,
absolutely classic,
A voice that an angel would love,
a voice that is way above,
A perfect tone & pitch,
vocals so potent & Rich,
A voice like this without a music contribution is
absurd,
how could a voice unlike any other be unheard,
The world deserves to hear every heavenly word,
a talented voice deserves appreciation,
It is one of gods gifts & creations,
Talent trumps all,
we have to walk before we can crawl,
let your voice & actions stand tall,
Never underestimate the power of sound,
a powerful voice can change your life around,
Rags to riches struggle to riding sensation,
a talented voice can lead a nation.

~Rose That Grew From Concrete 2~

Some may never witness,
a true struggle of rags to riches,
They may never understand the struggle,
never will they be able to match your hustle,
life can be a puzzle,
remain humble,
But be confident in nature,
success comes much later,
but first comes danger,
this a chance of success & failure
No mater life deadly foes,
or its various highs & lows,
Nobody can walk in the shoes of the Rose,
as it grows,
Thru the tough concrete,
just so it's journey can be complete,
Dreams remain intact,
Rose hopes to make a lasting impact,
Dispute the tough condition,
the rose is on a mission,
Don't focus on the enemy,
focus on growth & prosperity,
be a rarity,
life isn't a about popularity

it's about growth & reigning supremacy,
Rose overcoming any obstacle successfully,
Rose defined by its quality,
will forever live on in longevity,
with a one of a kind legacy.

Chapter Nine

Success Ladder

~ *Biggest Motivation*~

What guides you,
what motivates you,
what makes you go the extra mile,

Is it love,
is it lust,
is it trust ,

Is it for a better life,
is it for your health,
is it for the money,

Is it for your family,
is it for your kids,
is it for you & yourself only,

Never lose sight,
remember why you fight,
continue to do good & do what's right,

Let your positive be bigger than your negative,
don't be sensitive,
remain competitive,
never lose sight of your motive.

~From Ordinary to Extraordinary~

When two powerful forces combine,
they create greatness,
greatness in the form of two,
greatness in the qualities they pass on,
greatness in the knowledge they teach,
greatness in the form of experience,
Parents are providers,
parents teach you right from wrong,
a motherly touch is important,
a fatherly guidance is essential,
a motherly love goes a long way,
a fatherly presence counts for everything,
nothing is more important than family structure,
Both play equal parts,
love your parents,
listen to your parents,
respect your parents,
no bond can match this comparison,
no bond can create such a beautiful creation,
parents are truly the best people on earth,
to my parents I just want to say,
to my parents thank you for all the sacrifices & help,
along the way,
parents are extraordinary.

~Incredible~

In life we encounter incredible individuals,
who overcome life struggles,
no matter the troubles,
These individuals work hard,
play their cards,
Never complain,
dispute the pain & strain,
these incredible people maintain,
So much style & grace,
always having a smile on their face,
You deserve love for days,
you deserve praise,
in multiple ways,
Incredible people with great abilities,
always handling their responsibilities,
Incredible people with great character traits,
truly amazing & great,
blessings are coming to your way just wait,
These individuals are a blessing never a burden,
shout out to this incredible person,
You are loved & appreciated,
you deserve to be congratulated,
Incredible people are respectable,
keep being incredible,
you truly are impeccable,
cut from a different cloth your exceptional.

~*Opportunity*~

Same opportunities other neglect,
others are praying for,

Some people just need one chance,
some people don't deserve one at all,

Opportunities may come once but never again,
some opportunities may come frequently & all the
time,

Opportunities should never be taken for granted,
tomorrow isn't always promised,

With opportunities there is no room for error,
one slip up could be costly,

You never know what a person can do with just one
chance,
a little bit of opportunity goes a very long way for
some but not everyone,

Those who work hard should be rewarded,
those who don't reap what they sow,

The choice is yours,
make the best of what you have.

~No Comparison~

One life to live,

make the best of life you have,

learn to laugh,

learn what makes you happy,

learn how to overcome,

no competition because life isn't a race,

Life is about what makes you happy,

no fear because the only thing to fear is God,

never let anyone effect your happiness,

never let depression cause you to sink below your
limits,

Don't beat yourself up over failure,

mistakes will be made,

success will come in time,

Never judge your life by other people standards,

to change the world,

we must first change ourselves,

God only made one you,

there will never be another of your caliber,

there is only one you,

Cherish yourself.

~*Ambitions Beyond Reality*~

Faith in yourself determines your success,
your motivation is what you got to reassess
The key is ambition,
life is ongoing transition,
we too quick to act first instead of listen,
We must gain our own rhythm,
develop our own successful system,
the key is wisdom,
potential is often hidden,
But it's not hard to find,
don't focus on the finish line,
focus on the grind,
Doesn't matter what the path is,
long as it brings you eternal bliss,
ask yourself "How bad do I want this"
It may take days, weeks & hours,
you will have doubters,
you will have Debby downers,
in life you got to learn how to adjust & counter,
People will laugh & mimic,
you will have a few critics,
Some will be skeptic,
but don't forget your destiny is epic,
dispute the path being hectic,
when you reach success you'll receive love from the
public,

Don't get lost in what others are thinking,
continue building,
success will be quite fitting,
They say your ambitions are dumb,
your ambitions will sound crazy to some,
but just wait till the success come,
Everyone will be looking crazy,
all because your ambitions a reality.

~24 Hours~

Each day we are blessed with time,
it is up to us to use it wisely,

Time is always on our side,
we just got to know how to manage it,

We all have the same 24 hours in a day,
we all possess opportunity & ability to be great,

Greatness is in all of us,
greatness is a skill that can be practiced & mastered,

The time you put in goes a long way,
no time put in can lead to being stagnant,

Put in time now,
results of your efforts will kick in later,

What will you do with 24 hours,
the time is yours & time is now.

~Definition of Success~

What is your definition of success,

let me guess,

Is it money or fame,

is it Hollywood stardom you look to attain,

money & accolades you try to gain,

Is it about trying to make a name,

is it about putting a smile on your face,

buying a mansion or a nice place,

Is it about awards & praise,

what keeps you striving for days,

Is it about receiving recognition,

what's your definition,

is it to follow a family tradition,

Following a path of excellence,

are trying to set precedence,

is success maintaining intelligence,

what fuels your confidence & arrogance,

is success a matter of relevance,

Is your definition based on family,

is that what makes you happy,

Or do you want to look good in the public eye,

the question is a matter of why,

Is definition of success based on your health,

is it attaining wrath,

Success can be for anything or anyone,

can be for glory or happiness or income,

Can be for love,

or all of the above,

maybe you do it for yourself,

Maybe you do it for your wife,

or to provide a better life,

Maybe you do it for your children,

what's your mission,

Maybe you do it for your passion,

success is the ultimate satisfaction,

by it means necessary make it happen.

~Six Degrees of Separation~

We are unaware how our actions affect others,
our actions have an impact on not just us but
everyone around use,

Life can be funny sometimes,
our life scenario can play out in different ways,

Chain of events can affect many,
we're connected by friends, associates &
acquaintances,

Could be connected by faith or destiny,
it's a small world we live in,

You never know who is related to who,
you never know what others are going thru around
you,

Things that make us different,
also makes us similar in nature,

We are all unique with life experiences,
you never know who you may encounter in life,

Life has many coincidences,
we are all connected one way or another.

~Defeating The Odds~

Right now your doubting yourself,
right now you have no faith,
right now your down & out,

Right now your soaking in misery,
right now you feel all is lost,
right now you're in a negative state of mind,

You feel like you have no support,
you feel like you can't win,
you feel alone,

This thinking is only in your mind,
you are what you believe,
change your thinking & change yourself,

Today start a new change in your life,
rebuild a new faith & new confidence,
odds are now in your favor for the better,

You are amazing as can be,
you are powerful beyond measure,
you shall overcome & be victorious,

You are an unstoppable force,
your faith can't be matched,
your spirit can't be crushed,

Your blessed in many ways,
you're in blissful paradise,
your happiness matters,

You are strong minded,
you are positive & wise,
you have a strong support system,

You will accomplish your goals & more,
you are a winner,
you will overcome the odds.

~Support System ~

Never forget about the ones who were there from the beginning,
never forget who held you down when you wasn't Winning,

Never forget who erased that frown,
never forget who stayed down,

Never forget those that uplifted,
never forget those that knew you were gifted,

Never turn your back or burn bridges,
never forget who loved & accepted all your flaws & weirdness,

Never betrayed you & never lied,
always on your side & down to ride,

No matter the disagreements the love remained,
thru it all your support system never complained,

Always there providing knowledge, support &
wisdom,
thank god for your support system,

Your support system is crucial,
in life your support system will be useful,

You support system will always be truthful,
the love & support will always be mutual,

Shout out those who helped from day one,
shout out to those who helped you overcome,

Support system keeping you strong,
with good support system you can never go wrong.

~Stay Striving~

Stay striving is more than words,
stay striving is a way of life,

It's a movement of life & determination,
it's movement of positive actions & thoughts,

Stay striving isn't just in the mind,
stay striving revolves around the spirit,

Stay striving is a positive attitude towards life & the
situations that follow,
stay striving is more than a self-fulfilling prophecy,

The key is to look at the glass as half full vs half
empty,
the key is progressing towards goals & positive
actions,

Stay striving keeps the mind focused,
stay striving keeps actions heartfelt,

Stay striving til you reach the sky,
stay striving til you cross the finish line,

Stay striving will take you a long way,
stay striving is a way of life.

Chapter Ten

Expressions

~if Heaven Had Visiting Hours~

Instead of memories & flowers,
what if heaven had visiting hours,
Instead of having memories to reflect
what if we could reconnect,
What if we could have a sit down & talk,
or lounge around or take a walk,
What if we could spend the night,
what if you could hold that loved one tight,
What if you didn't have to cry
if heaven had visiting hours you could just stop by &
say hi,
No more struggle & grieving,
if heaven had visiting hours you could spend the
evening
Imagine if we had the chance to visit,
to be around our loved ones spirit,
Imagine just be in our loved ones presence,
just being among them in the heavens,

Just imagine all the endless encounters,

if only heaven had visiting hours.

~*Proud Of You*~

We always quick to point out the negative,
rarely do we acknowledge the positive,
We too quick to criticize,
instead of sympathize,
when will we realize,
Hating blocks our own blessings,
hating creates our own bad settings,
We have to learn to say congratulations,
celebrate the heat occasions,
never let anyone success be your frustrations,
Moved your family out of the hood,
then it's all good,
Got a job interview lined up,
best wishes to you & good luck,
Feeding your family trying to survive,
moving up the corporate ladder to thrive,
bought your wife a brand new car to drive,
Making good grades,
improving character traits,
Single parent handling your business,
providing for your kids every Christmas,
No matters if your goals are big or small,
shout out to you all,
Breaking old habits & starting brand new,
just so you know I'm proud of you.

~Secrets to the Grave~

Some secrets never see the light of day,
some secrets never leave the mouth,

Secrets often die with the individual,
the final resting place is grave,

We all have secrets in our closets,
some we are embarrassed to share,

Secrets are meant to be shared with the world,
secrets are supposed to go to the grave only,

Some secrets are so close to the heart,
nobody could ever get close to knowing,

Some secrets are special,
some secrets touch us emotionally & touch our
hearts,

Secrets can be between two people or many people,
not many people view a secret the same way,

Secrets can bring forward a dark past full of
memories,
secrets let us know what we done & how we
overcame,

Having secrets comes down to trust,
some secrets can destroy lives,

Secrets can never be dug up,
secrets reveal truths & lies,

Secrets have deep meanings,
leave secrets where they belong,

Secrets are not everyone business,
loose lips sink ships,

No matter how life plays out,
no matter what your secret is save with me.

~A Strong Rare Woman~

Rare kind of woman both inside & out,
your what a great woman is all about,
Thru adversity you remained positive,
your spirit & personality is addictive,
Nobody can match your determination,
woman of the year you got my nomination,
together you're the perfect combination,
Your wise,
you're the ultimate prize,
I don't know what's wrong these guys,
they must be blind,
To your amazing qualities,
they must be blind to your capabilities,
you always handle your responsibilities,
You are cut from a cloth that is special,
nobody is on your level,
your both an angel,
and a rebel,
You are loved to the highest degree,
top of the line your marquee,
the world may not see,
All that you do & have been accomplishing,
in my opinion your truly astonishing,
Salute to you & toast to the occasion,
from me to you this is my dedication.

~Statistics~

Some men & women aren't worthy,
thou shall not sex every man or woman on earth,

Sex is pure intimacy of the soul,
sex partners tell an untold journey of self,

It's not necessarily the number that is bad,
it's the quality that matters,

Self-worth & sex go hand & hand with one another,
sex change our lives in ways we never imagined,

Sex brings us many thrills & worries,
with the right person sex brings satisfaction,

Sex comes with pleasure & fantasies,
sex comes with dangerous consequences,

Sex with the wrong one can be devastating,
your sex partners can tell story of self,

Ladies every man doesn't deserve to see you naked,
your body is the most precious temple,

Fellas be careful with sowing your wild oats,
it's ok to have standards & self-worth,

There are no double standards with sex,
we all go thru the same consequences,

Statistics rarely lie,
be aware of who you're dealing with,

It's not always about statistics,
it's about awareness of self.

~ *Flashes of Brilliance*~

There is talent in all of us,
it just has to be seen & found,

Once found it has to be crafted,
hard work & talent go blend together,

In your later years you'll accomplish a lot more,
as of now your maturing & discovering yourself,

Individual growth is key to progress in life,
evolution is a must for everything we do,

Some will see their talent early some will see it late,
but it is there & you will discover it,

In our prime we start to invest in our craft,
brilliance starts to come to life,

Our greatness wasn't born yesterday,
it's been building since birth,

Don't rush the process of yourself,
time reveals any & everything,

You may not see now,
but there is greatness in you.

~*Cure*~

Too many lives lost to diseases,

as statistics increases,

There is no limit to which cancer reaches,

we need more then speeches,

More than a classroom that teaches,

truthfully we all need Jesus,

We need a new discovery,

quickly & in a hurry,

lord have mercy,

We need a breakthrough,

a smart scientific guru,

who can solve the issue,

so cancer can discontinue,

We need new studies,

cancer is causing way too many tragedies,

cancer is destroying way too many families,

These are issues we no longer have to endure,

we need a cure,

No matter if it's AIDS or any other type of cancer,

we need a cure, solution or better yet an answer.

~ Remarkable~

Single parent determined & motivated,

smart & very well educated,

to you this is dedicated,

Getting done by any means,

you are the embodiment of a queen,

Your life should inspire many,

you make the most out of every penny,

You work hard & strive,

you know how to make it & survive,

You are magnificent with a great heart,

as a good woman you play your part,

Nothing can measure up to your spirit,

you are a woman that is truly gifted,

A friend like you,

is a dream come true,

You make the impossible more than possible

the way you carry yourself is incredible,

you are not replaceable

Your personality is impeccable ,

you are remarkable.

~Future Outlook~

Your future can be bright,

Your future can be nonexistent,

your future revolves around the present,

your future matters,

Every decision effects your future,

the past can come back to haunt you,

being stagnant slows you down,

looking ahead takes the present for granted,

looking back too much hurts you,

The past is never at rest,

the present can always be changed,

future outlook is always shifting,

the key is to be consistent,

the key is to learn from mistakes,

the key is to stay focused,

Learn from the past,

prepare for tomorrow,

Enjoy the gift of today.

~Love Vs Like~

Love remains true & comes thru,

like only goes half way,

love creates a special feeling,

like creates a smile,

Love is a beautiful feeling,

like is full of happiness & laughs,

love is more than sex it's forever,

like is a bond similar to friendship,

Love accepts flaws & all,

like only tolerates it,

love is for an eternity,

Like is for now,

love doesn't die,

like can change with time,

love vs like both are acceptable,

one is for now the other is for a lifetime.

~*Somebody Understands* ~

When your down & out,

when you need a shoulder to cry on,

somebody is there that understands,

When your depressed,

there is somebody that understands,

Having a bad day,

lost your job or relationship,

there is somebody that understands,

Just got cheated on,

got a secret you want to reveal,

there is somebody that understands,

want to just sit & talk,

go for a walk or drive,

There is somebody that understands,

feeling horrible about life,

there is somebody who understands,

you are never alone,

There is somebody here for you,

never lose faith,

you will be uplifted,

trust me somebody understands.

~Naked Truth~

it's funny how life goes,
we have sky highs & pitfall lows,
We spent so much time together,
close as we want to be thru any weather,
Sneak around & do anything,
we are one another's everything,
Kissing, touching, rubbing,
we was always into something,
We was cool & slick,
I was your dude & you were my chick,
let's not forget,
I wanted to love, lick & give it to you the dick,
We found our self alone,
no condoms so I couldn't make you moan,
You were absolutely lovely & pretty,
I wanted to take your virginity,
I guess it wasn't meant to be,
I messed up that possibility,
Some years I thought you were mine,
I was never afraid to cross that line,
Soon got into a relationship with another guy,
you both were the apple of each other eye,
Things happened that we wouldn't believe,
I should have been there more in your time of
need,

I wanted to escort to every club & event
you were heaven sent,
I wanted to protect you from any harm,
I love your personality & flawless charm,
We both found ourselves in messed up situation,
but I still loved you with fascination,
We made each other horny,
loved each other strongly,
we have an unfinished story,
Life can be strange at times,
we making each other happy isn't a crime,
We put the ship in relation,
we are god's creation,
Nobody can stop us,
in God we trust,
Sex you the best way I can,
sex on beach of jet like sand,
I rather it just be us two,
your my wifey I'm your boo,
I love you,
Forever I'll catch you & have your back,
one day I'll put a ring on your finger I promise
you that,
Life can go any kind of way,
I got so much to say,
Nothing could affect you & me,
may the truth set us free.

~Smile Forever~

After a breakup don't be bitter,
instead get better,

Don't be mad or upset,
have respect,

Don't look at the relationship as a burden,
look at it as a blessing,

Don't look at the breakup as failure,
look at it as a lesson learned,

Don't try to get even,
just move forward,

Hold no grudges,
just wish them all the best,

Don't stalk their social media,
distance yourself to better yourself,

Don't get down about yourself,
better things are ahead,

You will smile again,
right now go for what makes you happy,
.

When the time comes best believe,
you will Smile forever.

~The Last Goodbye~

We meet people at the worst possible times,

often things work out other times not,

we can't control how will feel,

only how we act & pursue,

actions speak louder than words,

We grow at different paces of life,

I may grow faster

you may grow slower,

neither pace is right or wrong,

We grow at our own,

when we met it was bliss,

we connected as friends,

I liked you & vice versa,

We talked more & more,

I never once led you on,

never once did I toy with your heart,

never once did I take your feelings for granted,

Never once did I use you,

if anything we cherished each other,

talked for long hours,

your problems were my problems,

I was there every second,

I balanced you & a developing career,

all you wanted was a relationship,

I wasn't ready for one at the time,

I told you this repeatedly,

you thought you could change my mind,

you ended failing but being mad at me,

But I never told you to stay,

I never stopped you from dating,

I never was jealousy or angry,

I fully supported all your actions,

When I came into my own your support was greatly
appreciated,

maybe I wish somethings were different,

but you made the decision to stay,

just because you weather the storm don't mean you
get rewarded,

you had a choice to stay or leave,

Even when you had a relationship it was all love,

no hate only blessings,

you even said you wouldn't turn your back on me,

future would prove you wrong,

you did one last favor,

then you moved forward,

No love lost,

I wish you all the best,

in the end we both got what we wanted,

you got a relationship plus more,

I found myself & now prospering,

one day we will cross paths again,

but for now this is the last goodbye.

~Levels to Love~

It's levels to love,
it's a difference between loving you today & loving
you forever,
you can possibly love three people in three different
ways,
You can have many emotions for the ones you love,
feelings can exist for many,
but in life you can only choose one,
Life puts us in crazy situations,
from confusion to love triangle,
from numbness to mixed emotions,
life is full of surprises,
love has so many levels,
Some are easy to tell,
other are unexplainable,
love can be simple but complex,
love is sweet but toxic,
We all aren't on the same levels,
love isn't always equal,
passion isn't always mutual,

the right kind of love is truly beautiful,

it's hard to know where you stand,

love hurts in so many ways,

It's levels to love,

high risk equal high rewards,

an equal love is a great love.

Chapter Eleven

Journey of Life

~How To Know Yourself~

Knowing Yourself is very important,
we all need positive reinforcement,

First off who are you,
what do you love to do,

What makes you happy,
what makes you sad & angry,

What's your goal that your trying to accomplish,
what do you love & cherish,

Be determined & believe,
know that any & everything you can achieve,

You will experience trial & error,
but you will also get much better,

Uplift your self-esteem,
establish a support team,

Don't be cocky or arrogant,
remain true & excellent,

Remember why you do it in the first place,
always keep a smile on your face.

~*Fearless*~

Be ferocious in pursuing your endeavors,
never be afraid to take extreme measures,

Don't overthink,
stand up under pressure don't sink,

Maintain your courage,
apply your knowledge,

Maneuver thru adversity,
show growth exponentially,

Ignore procrastination,
focus on your destination,

Fear no struggle or nobody,
make your dreams a reality,

Leave your critics speechless,
be fearless.

~Trust issues~

Where did the trust go,
how do you let the actions show,
why does trust slowly grow,

Trust is in the mind frame,
trust is hard to gain,
trust lost easily damages the brain,

Broken trust can burn bridges,
ruin structure & business,
once broken it's hard to get forgiveness,

Trust is never to be taken for granted,
trust can be built on habit,
trust can be broken or expanded,

Trust comes down to patience & virtue,
know your value,
fix & adjust your trust issue.

~People Person~

People always wonder why,

people rather stay private,

some people dodge the public eye,

drama free is a peaceful climate,

no conversation just hi & bye,

Some people aren't loud they quiet,

some people prefer to be,

laid back in chill mode,

way of life is drama free,

quiet people live by a code,

Some people don't want to deal with mess,

it's way better to be around positively,

some people don't got time for the stress,

Nobody got time for negativity,

people want blessing not burden,

people want to live happy & blissfully,

a lot of men & women aren't a people person.

~Attraction isn't A Choice~

We can't choose who we have feelings for,

we can't just turn our attraction on & off,

feelings need to be addressed,

We just can't ignore the elephant in the room,

it's ok to love someone,

it's ok to lust after someone,

these feelings are not wrong,

it's perfectly normal for all,

The more you fight the stronger it get,

attraction is a beautiful force,

attraction brings two people together,

Attraction levels differ based on the individual,

attraction is in our mind,

attraction is powerful magic,

attraction rarely dies just remains stagnant,

attraction can increase or decrease,

Time is the biggest indicator,

attraction isn't just based on what we see,

attraction is based on what we feel,

when it comes to attraction we don't have a choice.

~Intentions~

Individual intentions can be good,

individual intentions can be bad,

We differ in upbringing & background,

some intentions bring good to all parties,

some harm everyone involved,

There is always a motive,

there is a method to the madness,

play your cards the best way possible,

take your time,

Think wisely & accurately,

it's a sucker born every minute,

but wise one born every second,

you don't have to play the fool,

never second guess yourself,

Bad choices have a domino effect,

get second opinions & thoughts,

never go into any situation blind,

Read before you react,

when it comes to intentions trust your gut instinct.

~*Miscommunication*~

I go left & you go right,

I cherish the day & you love the night,

I go down & you go up,

just my luck,

what do you expect,

I accept,

But you simply reject,

in the end we never connect,

I'm from Mars your from Venus,

I thought I was your strength but I'm your weakness,

I go fast you go slow,

we never on the same path or flow,

I aim for top you go for the bottom,

You think I'm ok I think I'm awesome,

you want what we have to die but I want it to blossom,

This back & forth cause frustration,

what's with all the miscommunication,

No matter how much we try to connect or engage,

we never on the same page.

~New Career Field~

You getting up there in age & now your
confused,
you don't know what path to pursue,
What career to do,
with bills overdue,
Your current job cause you misery,
you deserve to be happy,
not feeling crappy,
Maybe you want to be a teacher,
maybe a church preacher,
maybe a motivational speaker,
Possibly a drug dealer,
maybe neither,
But this current job isn't cutting it,
you want to quit,
this isn't a midlife crisis,
You just want to feel alive,
you want to thrive,
not barely make it to survive,
Not live paycheck to paycheck,
try something new to get your get wet,
plan in motion now you all set,
now it's time to burst a sweat,

don't stop till it's your last breath,
Put out multiple applications,
look deep into your imaginations,
do a self-examination,
Be inspired,
you are to be admired,
nothing beats those words " you're hired"
It's great to finally persevere,
congrats now enjoy your new career.

~*Purpose*~

Before you think about ending your life,

think of everyone who loves you,

think of everyone cherish you,

get bullied isn't fun,

you will overcome,

Getting judged for who you are,

your unique & continue to raise the bar,

your more then on par,

you come so far,

Imagine the roads you will conquer,

you got promises to honor,

it's time for you to prosper,

No need to commit suicide,

your more than greatly qualified,

With unbelievable upside,

you got greatness to provide,

You've been great since birth,

you have a purpose on this earth,

You got what it takes,

God doesn't make mistakes.

~Face Mask~

You are what you feel,

today it's the real you we reveal,

No need for makeup tips,

or the latest glamour on lips,

No more eyebrows on fleek,

no more make up on your nose & cheek,

Your more than the make up on your face,

you have original style & grace,

As your beauty products double in amounts,

it's your inside that counts,

Ignore the celebrities,

it's all about you & your personality,

Your more than Almay,

ignore what the commercials say,

Your more then cover girl,

you're the most beautiful woman in the world,

Put the make-up away,

I want you to know your beautiful each & every day,

No matter the blemish or scar,

you are amazing just the way you are.

~Achievements~

We win together as team,

we can all achieve our dream,

we can all reign supreme,

I'm going to admire your talent,

support your advancement,

never will you be stagnant,

I won't hate behind your back,

I will motivate & keep you on track,

it's not a race,

I will motivate you to keep up the pace,

Give you lots of praise,

encouragement for days,

your self-esteem I will raise,

We win as a state,

we can all be great,

You get support whether you known in the city,

or underground or indie,

I don't discriminate,

I rather uplift & motivate,

I'll acknowledge your ability,

congratulate you on your opportunity,

Support you in the community,

it's all about unity,

No matter our disagreements,

I wish you best in your achievements.

~*Before The Casket Drop*~

I want to make it to the top,
shake hands with famous legends,

Take pictures in beautiful locations,
attend make it wish foundations,

I want a big house with wife & kids,
a fish tank with pool table,

I want to make love to my dream girl & make her toes
curl,
she is the most important woman in my world,

I want to go on shopping sprees & not look at the
price,
I want my kids to have any & everything,

I want a big wedding for my wife,
I want a happy & blessed life,

I want to propose & do it big,
I want to drop classics,

I want success & recognition,
I want my own show on television,

I want the best for my family & friends,
I want to give back to my community,

I want the world to know my name,
I want to be one of the best in the game,

I see the path in front of me,
I won't give up till the casket drop.

~*Beyond Blessed*~

A roof over your head,

food on the table,

you are beyond blessed,

Ability to walk,

ability to drive,

you are beyond blessed,

In school working towards a degree,

at work moving up the ladder,

you are beyond blessed,

Family & friends still living,

pets still breathing,

you are beyond blessed,

Money in your pocket,

heart still beating right,

you are beyond blessed,

You opened your eyes this morning,

any day above ground,

you are beyond blessed.

~Open Mic Night~

Since I was a kid I loved to write

tonight is the night,

when the lights are on I shine bright,

I got to make sure my poetry is tight,

must make sure my wardrobe is right,

Wearing my good cologne,

poetry is in my bone,

tonight I make my name known,

Can't worry about who is in attendance,

I have to make a grand entrance,

make the crowd respect my presence,

Use my poetic words as a deadly weapon,

time to move the audience,

grab the microphone with confidence,

this poetic dominance,

Check one two,

Bryan Wesley here to offer something new,

this is from me to you,

Kicked a hot poem set the stage on fire,

I'm a poet & a writer,

I'm just here to take you higher,

Uplift you from your fears,

my voice is music to your ears,

The crowd erupted with noise,

you can feel the passion in my voice,

I step down to a standing ovation,

so many hi fives & admiration,

Years earlier I thought my craft & skills were absent,

tonight really open my eyes to my talent,

Tonight was just the beginning,

lord willing,

Maybe I'll go on to do great things,

we'll see what life brings,

I hope the world see that I'm gifted,

time is now sky is the limit.

Bonus Poems

Facebook Edition

~Sex On The Beach~

Let me ease your stress, introduce you to a place of
magnificence,
you've been so humble and full of patience,
it's time to reward you with a tropical Vacation,
No calls or text, just me treating you Best,
to submerge your depression in the sea,
I won't stop till your happy take off your shoes and
let your feet feel the sand,
enjoy the scenery of the land,
Play in the water, lets wrestle,
kiss & make a sand castle, let that body of goddess
be shown,
recognition of your elegance isn't wrong,
baby you grown, but now that we on this beach it's
on,
My destination is to each & every part of your
erogenous zone,
I don't care who witness, body is a temple let your
Work of art exhibit,
Straight undressing, body caressing,
sex education follow the lesson,

Don't Overthink,

let your inhibitions sink,

So much fun in sun,

X marks the spot when I'm done,

watch as the water drip, sensational love making as the moan and bite your lip, you stare at me in a daze, as I captivate and amaze, pleasure and satisfy you in multiple ways,

Baby I'm the best,

may be other fish in the sea but you're the only ultimate catch,

Vacation of fun & hot sex, by any means necessary, Doggystyle, Reverse Cowgirl, and of course Missionary, Body is drug & I'm overdosing,

Lick you ,stroke you from fast to slow motion,

Devour that fine meal of pussy lean cuisine,

True Black love is the finest thing,

I turned fantasy to reality from fiction into fact,

a day of fun and hot sex till you climax,

paradise is where we at, kissing you as we watch the sunset.

~Fuckin vs Making Love~

Fuckin is straight to the point, no B.S
Erases stress,
Puts you to rest,
Make you tap out or quit,
If you can feel your legs he don't deserve a
sandwich,
Hitting your spot, touching your zone,
After climax you both get dressed on your own,
Then head home,
Alone.
Making love is fulfilling, Pleasurable, Passion
meets wild sex,
Sweat dripping, leg shaking, heart beating out
your chest,
Love making isn't always slow,
because a man who know,
Will make you smile, bite your lip and curl your
toe,
You deserve the best,
Before & after sex
Relax under cuddle weather,
Couple that laugh together, stay together,
A REAL MAN puts in effort & work,
To show you your worth, cherish you as God's
gift to earth,

Being Spontaneous & unpredictable go a long way,
Switch up the words u say,
Fuck her like this, make love to her the next day,
Fuckin clinches the sexual craving like fast food,
Love making is a wine & dine plus setting the mood,
A real man going to teach you,
Lead you,
Spread your legs & have a feast with you,
Value & need you
Lil boys want to just chill,
To have a little thrill,
Which ever you prefer and pick,
Always value yourself over pussy & dick,
Fellas choose personality over Ass,
Pick the treasure never the trash,
Ladies pick personality over swag,
Pick the man who'll make a good husband or dad,
Make sure he treats you as a lady,
Never sex a man you can't call in case of an emergency,
Remember it takes two,
But the ultimate choice is up to you.

~Rachet Mentality~

So much ignorance I can't believe, It's so much you can achieve,
but instead you wear your Rachetness on your sleeve,
in your mind your logic goes in reverse, is it a proud statement or a curse, it's your esteem & integrity that suffer the worst,
You Can "TURN UP" but your priorities remain down,
LOOK AT HOW YOU SOUND,
You can "ROLL UP"
But your maturity remains complacent & never grows up, It remains Stuck,
I guess these the consequences of not giving a fuck,
Fellas won't put job applications, but attend a Jordan Release, Not there for your kids birthday but chasing hoes in the streets,
Stand up & be a real man instead of a REAL NIGGA,
Fight your battles instead of trying to pull a trigga,
You rather fuss & fight,
BOY GET RIGHT,
You rather run game, lie and penetrate,
You rather ask "CAN I PULL UP" instead of asking her on a DATE,
out here Fuckin & making lots of babies,
You think you a real man because you impregnated multiple ladies,
Fuckin & cheating must be fun,

A real man is LOYAL to one,
Don't get me started on some of you chicks,
Chasing & Fuckin no good dicks,
Fuckin, sucking a nigga daily, nightly, weekly,
But you can't call him when you have an emergency,
Sticking birds in your pics,
I guess you don't give a shit,
Well you ain't shit, what a travesty,
far from classy,
In the FAST LANE materialism is what you chase,
You clock in more HOURS in the club then your
workplace,
catering to dick instead of your kids...what a
disgrace,
I guess that's life,
No excuses that don't make it right,
get it together it's not a good look, change those
tweets, Instagram & posts on Facebook,
When your ship sunk, or you in a slump,
Rise & strive to get out your ratchet funk,
Upgrade your reality,
Get out your rachet mentality.

~Friends With Benefits~

We share likes, dislikes and common ground,

Dependent, True, loyalty we always stayed down,

Only smiles no frowns,

Like true friends there was the good & bad,

The times I was there when you was sad,

The times I pissed you off and you was mad,

But like friends we put it behind us in the past,

But at last,

We see a new dilemma,

Let us address, The subject of sex,

And what comes next,

Do we Fuck without passion,

Do we skip the Romance & jump straight to the
action,

When finished do we chunk deuces or cuddle after
smashing,

Will you look at me different after you grip the
sheets,

Back to back climax as you reach your sexual peak,

Will I still be a friend or will I make you weak,

A month ago we was just chilling,

Now after sex we caught feelings,

Nothing now will be the same,

We should of known its levels to this game,

Rule one only fuck,

A person you trust

Be careful of lust,

And protection is a must,

Rule two Be honest,

Communication is key,

Don't be controlled by the dick or pussy,

Rule three,

Don't compromise you,

Be safe and aware of who, you dicking down or giving pussy to.

~Black Is Beautiful~

With all the images on TV,

Depicting their ideal of beauty,

Dividing us with Photoshop tricks & foolery

The beauty of a woman isn't based on her look,

Its Skin deep not what u see on Instagram or

Facebook,

It's not in the Makeup,

We as African Americans need to wake up,

Nowadays we'll do anything for attention or to be

seen,

Beauty isn't in the Almay, Covergirl or Maybelline,

Long as your personality a ten,

The true beauty is within,

Forget what's said on B.E.T

ignore the videos on MTV

Forget what is said in songs

Dark, Yellow, Red bone,

Black is beautiful in any skin tone,

Forget their color struck view,

Nobody defines you,

Preference or Color struck

There's a fine line,

Ladies u are more than your goodies or that ass

Behind,

but some are simply blind,

To your personality or your intelligent mind,

Make your money do what you got to do,

Never forget where you came or heading to,

Gentleman be men but well extinguished,

Be ambitious,

Climb the ladder of success,

Strive to be your best,

And handle whatever adversity comes next ,

Together united we stand formidable,

It's understandable,

Black is beautiful every way imaginable.

~Cuffing Season~

As Winter comes near,

It's that time of year,

Where summer heat cools down,

Cuddle weather as leaves & snow hit the ground,

As the weather change,

Men & woman are on the hunt for their "Boo Thang"

Ladies dressing in leggings & tights,

Looking for Mr. right, just to keep warm at night,

Some are searching for sex or a buddy,

Some will get there wish while others aren't so lucky,

Be happy with your mate,

You never know the fate,

All relationships are give & take,

Marshmallows with hot chocolate under cool
weather,

Sex, holidays, video games together,

Thanksgiving feast, cruising looking at Christmas
lights,

Making snow men and having snowball fights,

Black Friday shopping, getting sick catching colds,

Watch TV ,play fights never getting old,

Under the mistletoe sharing kisses,

On December 25 fulfilling Christmas wishes,

Bringing the new year in,

Valentine's day kissing, sexing, over & over again

Enjoying sweet taste of Valentine's day candy,

This season you were treated quite fancy,

But what was important was you being happy,

It's safe to say cuffing season was more satisfactory.

~Breast Cancer Awareness~

October the month known for so many things,

Human life is roller coaster that brings,

Joys of today hopefulness for tomorrow,

Also brings pain, hurt and sorrow,

If you know anybody with breast cancer hold them
close,

Give them love and be there the most,

Life can be so unfair,

Show them that you care,

Be aware,

Get checkups and see the early signs,

1 and 8 women will be diagnosed in their lifetime,

Many are walking around,

Locally in your city & town,

That need checkups & mammograms,

With breast cancer affecting a percentage of the
women population,

it's a must we treat, care, support & offer donation,

Support the Pink ribbon with pride,

Let us never lose stride,

We will survive,

Keep hope alive,

Cancer may affect the body but never mind & spirit,

May my words bring joy to those who need it,

Remain positive & let the mind & spirit be pure,

Keep the faith and remember God is the cure.

~Thirsty vs Flirting~

In this day & age,

Men/Women seem to be on a different page,

We get confused in our views & ways,

"Are they interested " or searching for a quick lay,

Is the question we often ask & ponder,

It's no wonder,

Is he/she thirsty or is this flirtation,

Is this person searching for only sexual relations ,

Or interested beyond admiration,

& looking for nice dinner date in isolation,

Thirsty means going beyond desperate measures,

To satisfy your illicit pleasures,

To fulfill your little thrill,

Lust is what u strongly feel,

Thirsty is searching for satisfaction of one u don't know,

You don't want a relationship to possibly grow,

Thirsty is ignoring all possible ramifications,

Aiming to please your own gratification,

Ignoring all the signs,

Inboxing him/her multiple times,

Between thirsty & flirting you been crossed that line,
What a crime.
Just because he/she say "Good morning " doesn't
make them thirsty,
that's just courtesy,
let's not forget to mention,
some women will sell they soul for attention,
Flirting is innocent, with subliminal hint,
It's not breaking the rules just a mere bent,
With a smirk or Mona Lisa smile,
Tone of voice with alluring style,
Actions subtle but the thoughts are wild,
Flirting doesn't rush,
Can happen with slightest bit of touch,
Thirsty is rush hour traffic on a rainy day,
Flirting is cruising thru life in simple enjoyable way,
Thirsty causes resistance,
Flirting is sincerity meets persistence.

~*The Art of Kissing*~

Look into my eyes tell me what do you see,
Close them as we kiss passionately,
Do you feel that?,
Butterflies moving how do you react?,
Heart pounding fast,
Enchanted kiss that will forever last,
A kiss yet delicate with so much meaning,
A kiss filled with emotions and feelings,
The forehead kiss innocent but very erotic,
Anxious tension borderline psychotic,
There is a certain level of skill to this logic,
Here is the inside trick,
Don't overthink just go for it,
Seize the flow,
Let that person know,
They matter most,
Look them in the eye & bring them close,
Move in slowly but surely,
No doubt kiss them confidently,
Bask in the moment of bliss,
Now you know the Art of the kiss.

~Life of a Single Parent~

Life has its Up & Downs,

Its smiles, cries, frowns,

but nothing beats the sights & sounds,

Of bringing a precious life into the world,

Whether its boy or girl,

Took 9 months of labor,

Looks identical to mom & dad so they favor,

Now here you are holding your bundle joy in your arms,

Promising them the world & protecting from harm,

But one minor thing is wrong,

Your precious joy may,

Raised in a single parent home,

So now you feel alone,

But it's no need to fear,

Family & friends & blessings will appear,

No need to shed a tear,

Your blessed beyond fortune,

ladies don't get that abortion,

Fellas take care of your responsibilities & fair share of the portion,

Sometimes you got to play both roles to provide needs,

It's not cheap with an extra mouth to feed,

Make your money by any means, to succeed,

Do what you got to do to get out of a financial funk,

If anybody judging u say to them "So which one of my bills u paying this month"

Pay check to pay check, Food stamps do what's best for you,

because at the end of the day u catering & nurturing for two,

Think positive you will not fail,

Shout out to the single father's as well,

Its hard finding a babysitter while you're working thru the day,

God will provide a way,

Strong will & independence will get you by,

You are not cursed but this is the ultimate blessing in disguise.

~*The Friend Zone*~

An attraction like no other,

But they only look at u as a sister or brother,

On your end the attraction has fully grown,

But theirs never change now you enter the friend zone,

You can look but don't touch,

Just the thought of them makes u smile & blush,

But you don't want to ruin or rush,

What yall have and built thru the years,

But you want to express how u feel,

Show them true love & show them something real,

But they probably won't feel the same,

Who's to blame.

Nobody sadly it's just part of the game,

Be a man/woman and say what's in your heart,

Make sure it's a journey u truly want to embark,

The friendship bridge is a tricky one,

But in the end you win some, you lose some,

You never know a person reaction,

Sometimes it comes down to chemistry & attraction,

A lack of personality or maybe passion,

Sometimes it comes down to that special "It Factor"

Acting on that friend could lead to marriage or worse disaster,

Maybe you'll get your chance someday,

And have your way,

Remember the knowledge I say,

If ever in the friend zone with no direction where to go,

Just know,

That happiness & the final outcome is in your hands,

Friend zone can be complicated to understand,

A tough dilemma to face,

The key is dodging the friend zone in the first place.

~*Marriage Material*~

Our ambition & perseverance to succeed,

We come across Men & Women of many breeds,

Some we encounter, want & need,

Whether destiny or fate,

We encounter potential mates,

Some are seasonal & play a part,

Some manage to steal our hearts,

Some hold our interest for a day,

Then there is the one who got away,

There are the ones who worked our nerves,

Said the unbelievable & absurd,

Left us breathless simply no words,

This thing we call life introduce us to sunshine & rain,

Joy & pain,

The right one will make you proud,

Give u butterflies & have u soaring above clouds,

Looking u in eye as they say the wedding vows,

Ladies the right man,

Will have a life goal with a plan,

He be there to understand,

Honest truth no games,

No pointing fingers placing blame,

You're the object of affection & your heart is to be obtained,

He'll give you respect,

Sacrifices & compromises in the middle ground will be met,

More than your body he'll respect your intellect,

Surprise you at your job with edible arrangement,

marriage material you'll think he is heaven sent,

Fellas with the right lady,

There is no maybe,

She'll be there with loyalty

Queen with admirable royalty,

She won't use you,

Or ride shotgun she'll pull right beside you,

And be like "Ready Boo"

She is a dream come true,

She don't got time for the games,

Marriage material reward her with ring & your last name.

~Death of Swag(D.O.S)~

As a man or woman always have confidence,
Take care of self & appearance,
Facebook stunting & Instagram pics,
In ya hottest fit,
But don't depend all on it,
Take pride,
But they better love or "like" you based on your
inside,
Jealous ones hate or despise,
Your happiness is to be mesmerized,
Whether you turning up or going Ham,
You aren't measured by how many "likes" you get on
Instagram,
Such an annoyance,
That we get judged by flamboyance
What's in our heart should value higher importance,
It is not what you wear,
But the confidence displayed makes em stop & stare,
Swag gains a step, but personality will take you a
mile,
The most beautiful thing a woman wears is her smile,

Some ladies rather be a "bag of money " or baddest bitch walking,

Let your success captivate the masses & your accomplishments do the talking,

Fellas don't be imprisoned by greed or wealth,

Best thing in life is health,

Be yourself,

The price of yourself has no amount,

Admire the exterior but its the inside that count,

Personality should get their attention,

Swag is just an extension,

That's worthy of an honorable mention,

Be different who cares if they laugh,

Pave your own path,

Everybody trying to be the same,

no twitter let's stop "Following " and lead for a change.

~Local Love~

Pursue your craft with passion,

Take a course of action,

No matter what avenue you pursue,

Do it for you,

Have a plan,

Be thankful of your Supporters & fans,

Your spotlight will grow & so will your mentions,

Some people will ignore you altogether,

Some will support you thru any weather,

Some will drive to your event or show,

Some will say "Maybe next time" or simply No,

But always keep your engine running on go,

One monkey doesn't slow, the show,

Your own city,

Often shows no mercy, or pity,

They either hate you or love you once you a celebrity,

They claim you changed, once you gain,

Notoriety & fame,

Some places support you & want to see you stand tall,

Sometimes your own city want to see you fall,

Some will admire your craft & ambitious passion,

Pay attention to action,

Not everyone is hater or supportive,

Be appreciative

Don't be jealous or filled with envy,

Stay Striving & fill your mind with positively,

Success is a sweet addiction to an ambitious fiend,

Support any & everyone following their dream,

To the locals seeing talent isn't hard,

Its growing in your own backyard ,

Support the youth on goals & paths they embark,

Support the photographers capturing Art,

Support businesses trying to upstart,

Support models exhibiting beauty & fashion,

Support authors with a writing passion,

Support local artists in the Booth,

Promoters are the truth,

Support local athletes going to college or pros,

Support anyone striving towards their goals.

~~ *Qualities of Leadership~~*.

Work ethic is the trait of a leader,

Strive for excellence at cost.

Determination guides a leader,

Goals help motivate leaders.

Teamwork surrounds a leader,

Sometimes we judged by how we lead others.

Clutch time is a leader best time,

Leaders are the people you can count on.

Excellence is what leaders commend,

Leaders make everyone around them better.

Courage is an amazing trait,

Those leaders are known for.

Integrity is a main component of a leader,

Leaders trust in others and believe in themselves.

These are the traits of a leader,

Leaders forever remain true.

~Quality Over Quantity~

One thing has to be understood,

From adolescence to adulthood,

It's not about how many,

Or having plenty,

It's about quality,

It's about being stable,

Having someone who is loyal & able,

More than capable,

Fellas the one lady who supports your dream,

Is the biggest supporter on your team,

Ladies the one Guy who you ignore,

Is the one Guy who supports you and more,

Look amongst you in your scenery,

Do you feel the energy,

Surround yourself with positively,

Ignore drama & negativity,

Quality maintains its integrity,

Last the test of time so it has longevity,

You can have a team of hoes,

But how many support your ambitious goals,

How many using you on the low,

How many will stay & how many will go,

Only time will show,

Relationships of many kind,

Go thru evolution in time,

It's not about the size, bulk, quota or amount,

It's the quality that count,

Those hardest to love need it the most,

Hold them close,

Hug your family & friends,

Ride with them till end,

If you have someone in your life you love show em every day,

Time passes but Quality of a great person never fades away.

~Insecure Dudes~

We as individuals are all born with different traits,

Our choices Good or Bad determine our Fate,

Our deepest flaws & insecurities we ignore,

Even though they are tearing us up at our inner core,

Ladies ever date that one guy,

He always question you on who, what, & why.

You both grown,

He sneak peeks & snoop thru your phone,

No matter the issue you're the one in the wrong,

He supposed to Love you,

But when he mad he threatens you,

Harms you,

Blames you for everything & gives you evil looks

He swear you Fuckin every dude on Facebook,

He makes you sad,

Blames you for everything in his Past,

Same drama every day nothing new,

He rather accuse you,

Fuss, fight, & argue,

Got you trapped feeling like you can't win,

Then he say "Bae I'm sorry" then repeat his actions

all over again,

Dear ladies start taking control,

The same shit gets old,

Be bold,

He better respect your mind, body & soul,

He better learn how to trust,

Or there won't be an "US"

If he can't treat u as equal or his better half,

Then exit I bet you'll have the last laugh.

~Clingy Chicks ~

Fellas ever meet that one woman so beautiful &
glamorous,

She seem so unreal & harmless,

Intoxicating & luxurious,

Too good to be true,

It all looks like the start of something new,

Until things start to go sour,

She start texting & blowing you up by the hour,

Constant "What you doing" texts its pure madness,

This clingy behavior is sadness,

She making life plans together in a short period of
time,

She may be fine,

But she is out of her mind,

No father figure of any mention,

Maybe that's why she needs so much attention,

She doesn't know how to give a person space,

Now She discussing kids & getting a place,

She head over heels & acting like a dog in heat,

She discussing Marriage, kids, getting our own place
all in one week,

This isn't love she strongly in lust ,

She forcing & trying to rush,

Try to let her down easy & bounce,

Now she showing up at your job unannounced,

She nonstop & won't quit,

She acting crazy & bipolar as shit,

Crazy part is she hasn't even received the dick,

Who saw all this coming,

Life is truly something,

Fellas pay close attention,

If you encounter a lady of such distinction,

Don't play with her heart,

Be honest from the start,

Don't lead her on or play with her mind,

Don't try to fuck,

Then wonder why she clingy & stuck,

If she isn't the one let her know,

Say "Goodbye " & let her go.

~It's Complicated~

There is a boundary line,

Between relationships of many kind,

These relations we can't explain,

They drive us insane in the brain,

One day we friends next we close as lovers,

But we give our intimate actions to others,

One day I'm a boyfriend next I'm like a brother,

Why do we give ourselves to everyone else instead
of one another,

Our confused minds wonder, Where do we stand,

Do we have a plan,

Are you my girl & am I your man,

What's our goal,

These games we playing getting old,

One minute we friends with a benefit,

Next we lovers with the candles lit,

Next it's no love or affection you hesitant,

Treatment like a stranger you never knew,

Then next u shooting me a text saying "Come Thru"

Then we Sex,

Get dress,

Then wonder "Damn What's Next"

Is this temporary are we Fuckin or love making,

Are we single as fuck or are we single but our hearts taken,

Hooking up or fooling around,

Am I just your rebound,

We laugh, we argue, we fuss,

Some situations aren't complicated the answer right in front of us,

But we blinded by love or maybe even lust,

Let's be honest this is no relationship,

This is merely convenience of a Situationship

Its amazing how what we had faded,

Damn how can something so simple end up being complicated.

~A Woman's Inner Freak~

A Beautiful Lady with style & Grace,

Confidence radiates off her face,

She can't be duplicated nor replaced,

Only man she desires is one who can match her pace,

She dominates with tremendous power,

Independent she making money by clocking in by the hour,

She the type that leave u wanting more,

There is a another side to her behind closed doors,

A side only her mate will get to witness,

In the bedroom she handles Business,

Let's not pretend,

Women are just as freaky as men,

She'll send freaky texts while you at your workplace,

Soon as you get home she'll put that pussy in your face,

When she horny she don't know how to act,

Biting her lip & putting scratches in your back,

Confident & bold

Sex with her never gets old,

She know how switch roles,

She know when to be submissive when need be,

But she loves to be dominated & fucked amazingly,

She doesn't want u to hesitate,

She likes men who lead & initiate,

Who isn't afraid to make her legs quiver & shake,

As a woman show her respect,

But as her mate spice it up & get her wet,

She wants her hair pulled, ass smacked, legs numb,

Don't be fooled her juicebox will leave you sucking on your thumb,

She is more than capable,

Knows multiple positions and is flexible,

she wants in bedroom, car, living room & on the kitchen table,

She is freak,

She put it down & put u to sleep,

You thinking you going to pipe her down,

But she left you speechless without a sound.

~Sex Therapist~

Allow me to introduce myself,

I'm your sex therapist & I'm here to enhance ya
sexual health,

Follow my every lyric,

Allow me to cleanse your mind & free your spirit,

Allow me to take you to a place you didn't know
exist,

Don't be afraid & don't resist,

I insist,

Blow you out like a birthday cake & make a wish,

Lay on this comfortable mattress,

I got matters to address,

First off baby you are blessed,

No contest,

No competition you put them all to rest,

What's that you say?,

You haven't had a man make love to you in a special
way,

They just smash & dash and go bout they day,

Baby girl I can't pretend,

Those fellas are boys not men,

a man hasn't never made you cum,

Energizer bunny he beat it like drum,

Its only so long you can fake it,

Till you make it,

Make him slow his pace,

Love making Marathon this isn't a race,

Control the flow,

Stroke you nice & slow,

Get you on all fours,

Multiple orgasms I promise you'll get yours,

What's the craziest sex you ever done,

Sex in broad daylight in the sun,

Sex in the backseat or on top of the hood,

In the woods,

Make damn sure he respect,

your intellect,

Then you can bless him with that wet wet,

Let out that inner freak,

Put that pussy on a man & put him to sleep,

Move that hand & let him go deep,

If you single,

Step out and mingle,

Sex takes two,

Never be afraid to try something new,

FWB or one night stand,

Strap up & be up front with a plan,

No shame, in your game,

The aim,

Is simply to please,

To succeed at satisfying your every womanly need,

Problems resolved,

Is that all,

You got an itch that needs to be scratched,

Facts,

Well undress and relax,

As your sex therapist I promise you the ultimate climax.

~Black Super Man~

Let me address the state of love in black America ,

thru the hoopla and hysteria,

one of a kind no replica ,

for the boyfriend position they may enlist,

many boys will be dismissed,

this position doesn't require much,

just a manly touch,

a man that can deliver in the clutch,

one that handles his responsibilities,

fearless & full of endless possibilities,

not playing games but is stable,

committed and faithful,

doesn't do nothing distasteful ,

in the relationship he is grateful,

you are his beautiful black queen

united to form a perfect team,

he'll erase your insecurities & raise your self-esteem,

your heart he'll redeem, he is the ultimate love

making machine,

he is the cream,

of the crop,

his love is nonstop,

he will spoil you rotten,

he is a good man with no other option,

question remains who are you?

your a black queen who prevails thru,

always remain true,

unbreakable striving remaining motivational,

no rookie you know the game you're a professional,

head held high & walking with confidence,

you make great choices with no fear of the
consequence,

together you and this man make a great pair,

reliable so he always there,

if you have this man in your life,

hold on to him tight & treat him right,

if you are without,

have no doubt,

he'll arrive soon,

bringing with him the stars & the moon,

the man with a plan,

every black queen deserves a black super man.

~Relationship Status~

In the beginning,

it's no predicting ,

how a person can have you grinning,

at the same time have you thinking,

of endless possibilities,

it seem like all your everyday activities,

revolve around that special mate,

as of late,

sexing, texting and movie dates,

they make you laugh plus they have other amazing
traits,

but hold up pump your brakes,

things aren't really clear,

the sweet actions in the beginning start to disappear,

you get confused and wonder is a relationship near,

inconsistent vibes & signals ,

are they in to the relationship or just the physical,

ladies some men start off gentlemen then you see
they assholes & egotistical,

gave you nothing but compliments now after pussy
they overly critical,

meanwhile ignoring your question "Nigga is we official"
went from good morning texts such as "good morning boo"
now acting like a stranger acting brand new,
fellas encounter that chick,
you click with,
in the beginning gave you butterflies and now she make you sick,
tried to talk to her & establish a relationship plan,
now you don't know where the hell you stand,
treat her like no other,
now she saying "Your like a brother"
ladies like a consistent man who treats them like the highest value,
love her and let sincere actions continue,
fellas like a lady they can trust,
loyalty a must,
a lady down to ride,
but can switch it up and pull up right along side,
not knowing where you stand makes a person feel lost & frustrated,

are we "Single" or "In a relationship" or is it complicated,

keep me updated,

what are the possibilities that we get upgraded,

you know what damn this consider yourself terminated,

between you and that special person,

if things worsen,

get rid of the stress & burden,

makes things clear so the status of the relationship won't be uncertain,

a relationship is a addition,

not a completion,

look in the mirror and love me, myself and I,

stay positive & with god you'll get by.

~Crabs in a Barrel Mentality~

As you start to blossom

on your road to stardom,

there are scum,

even in the place you originated from,

that want you to fail,

never to prevail,

your success they hope to derail,

never do they admire your ambitious trail,

they rather hate & despise ,

prey for your demise,

tear you down with rumors & lies,

word to the wise

they will overlook & ignore

as you strive for more,

they fake a smile & show up at your front door,

intruder alert,

last week you were treated as dirt,

a little success now they see you as God gift to the

earth,

know your worth,

don't let success get to your head,

remember the words that was said,

only god knows your journey ahead,

supporters will love it but your crabs will dread,

with success to gain,

just when you think you close to fame,

they pull you down & destroy your name,

denounce then hate or throw shade,

but your sun will rise & never fade,

only time they drive match yours is when they
dreaming,

no matter they methods of scheming,

remember my teaching,

when the crabs start reaching,

just continue striving & leading,

shine bright & never stop believing

cherish friends & family,

remember the crab mentality,

the come up was the beginning & your success will
be the grand finale.

~Black Super Woman~

In this sequel,

we soon discover an equal,

this deadly combination is lethal,

Together to make a power couple,

together they spell double trouble,

black super woman never does she stumble,

maintains order so her household never crumble,

Fueled by ambition,

trusting her intuition,

No ratchet can destroy her vision,

always making the right decision,

Provides a way,

steps in to save the day,

Nobody can break her spirit,

she is truly gifted,

as a friend she'll help you get uplifted

Always come thru & always reliable,

classy & desirable,

Holds her own,

never childish she is top notch grown,

She is a dream come true,

only hangs with a few,

She is more than meets the eye

sets her goals high,

doesn't need a guy,

Black super woman gets it done by any means,

shout out to the black queens,

Pays her own bills,

gets the job done with her superhero skills,

Provides for her kids,

nonsense she strictly forbids,

If she married with a ring,

she supports her king,

Wifey traits she possess,

the S on her chest,

isn't just super it's also success,

Black & beautiful,

exquisite & well suitable,

For this black queen you better make way,

black super woman is striving every single day,

Maintains her values & virtues,

fixes any and every issue,

black super woman is here to the rescue.

~That's Not Bae~

The State of dating,

Seems to be frustrating,

Not careful & the consequences can be devastating,

I think our generation needs educating,

How come guys aren't taking ladies on a date,

Why lie when you can give it to her simple & straight,

Because telling her what she wants to hear is the bait,

Till you get in her jeans,

By any means,

Girl after girl same old routine & Schemes,

He treats you like other chicks,

Feed you Bud light, Dick & Netflix,

It's funny how we try to brag,

But we ignore the red flags,

You are just pussy until proven wifey,

But he full of BS chances he upgrades you is unlikely,

Sex you in private,

He completes you so you feel delighted,

Better yet excited,

But he doesn't claim you in public,

Temptation you can't resist,

Sometimes he acts like you don't exist,

One minute you're the best,

Then next,

It's missed calls & him ignoring your text,

He is your weakness,

But rarely does he cause you any happiness,

Let me explain loud & clear,

BAE only telling you what you wanna hear,

You place him on a pedestal,

But he treats you terrible,

His BS is unbearable,

BAE want to share you with his homeboy,

Like you some toy,

Relationship is a 2 way street,

but BAE don't want to see you on your feet,

He wants you on your back & legs spread,

Thumbs down let them know that shit dead,

He never helps when you down on your luck,

All he trying to do is fuck,

He kept you guessing,

You thought he was a blessing,

But he was a burden & lesson,

You gave him the benefit of doubt,

Now you see it was BS coming out his mouth,

Develop zero tolerance,

Stop enabling & make him face the consequence,

And that's losing you,

Loving yourself is long overdue,

In your own eyes,

You're the prize,

Don't ignore the words I say,

No more excuses that's not bae.

~Black America~

Let's have an intervention,

And establish a sense of direction,

No race or gender is pure perfection,

But some issues are due for correction,

Maybe we will provide answers to our questions,

Let's begin,

Light skin vs dark skin,

Only in the black community,

Do we attack each other skin tone brutally,

Vicious and ruthlessly,

But truthfully,

God created us all beautifully,

2nd issue to address,

Why do we seem to obsess,

With materialistic possessions,

But downplay our artistic expressions,

How come we don't stick together,

Through whatever,

Why do we stand in line for Jordans to purchase,

But won't vote for change or purpose,

Why do we make each other feel worthless,

Why do we ignore positive but push negativity,

We question our masculinity,

Wipe away our pride & dignity,

I guess ignorance is shining blissfully,

Seems like we at war with our own kind,

It seems like when a woman speaks her mind,

She gets criticized,

We as black America got to learn how to mobilize,

The negativity we got to minimize,

In our community we got to specialize,

In restoring core values,

Tackle injustice & other major issues,

Educate our youth,

Spread knowledge & truth,

Black men don't be quick to pull the trigger,

Black men are kings not niggas,

Black women aren't bad bitches,

They are queens & princesses,

I'm not promoting anti-white,

Because every gender & skin color is blessed in its own right,

No matter your race I hope you shine bright,

This is no race war or battle,

Just leading by example,

Let's stop all the hate,

Black America let's be great.

Contact

Email- Bryan88Wesley@Gmail.com

Twitter – BryanWesley88

Instagram- Bryan_Wesley88

Facebook- Bryan Wesley (FanPage)

YouTube- BryanWesleyTV

SnapChat- Bryan88Wesley

Periscope- Bryan Wesley

Website Coming Soon- January 2016

www.ingramcontent.com/pod-product-compliance
Lightning Source LLC
Chambersburg PA
CBHW071948040426
42447CB00009B/1287